Forging Dynasty Businesses

Forging Dynasty Businesses

The Competitive Edge of Enduring Teams

Chuck Violand

Chuck Violand and the team at
Violand Management Associates, LLC
Trusted advisors to businesses in the
trades and service industries

BUSINESS EXPERT PRESS
Leader in applied, concise business books

This book is dedicated to the fearless and hardworking small business owners we've been privileged to work with through Violand Management Associates.

Description

People are one of the few remaining, reliable sources of sustainable, competitive advantage. Competitors will copy marketing strategies, and technology and process advantages will fade over time, but having the best people for your organization will turn customers into raving fans, allowing you to have a more enjoyable ride as you achieve your goals.

Most business owners give lip service to the mantra that people are our greatest assets, but how many really grasp the deeper implications of this? After all, people are listed on income statements as an expense (payroll) but are nowhere to be found under assets on our balance sheets.

This book provides the keys to unlock the fundamental elements of an organization that serve as the foundation for small businesses to perpetually attract and retain top talent—those who fit with the organization's culture and core values and who contribute to achieving the organization's goals.

Keywords

company culture; employee retention strategies; hiring; recruiting; retaining; competitive advantage; employer of choice

Contents

Preface

At Violand Management Associates, a significant part of the work we do with our clients is to track their financial performance. This allows the client to see firsthand the level of improvement they're experiencing as a result of our assistance. As with most small businesses, the single largest expense they have is payroll, so we watch these expenses very closely, working to make sure the client stays within firmly defined parameters while still meeting their business objectives.

As the years have gone by and the number of clients has increased, we have been able to identify certain patterns. One such pattern, in almost all cases, has been that the clients who pay their workers the best seem to perform better than the ones who insist on paying the lowest wages. Time and time again, we have seen companies that pay poorly suffer higher turnover, lower employee morale, lesser quality, and weaker financial performance as a result. Those clients appear to have proven what business guru Peter Drucker wrote about some years ago—that you can't build a profitable company on low-wage workers.

The topic of the growing disparity of income in the United States has gained a lot of attention, especially as it relates to competition in business. One such article was published in *Harvard Business Review*. In reading the article, it became clear how some very large, highly successful companies use income disparity as a strategy to compete even more successfully in their markets by employing the highest-paid workers. But this concept isn't limited to large, multinational companies. When we look at small business competition in just about any industry, a similar strategy can be seen.

In addition to increased demand for the products and services produced by small businesses, there are several other forces that place pressure on our ability to attract and retain talented workers. Three such pressures that stand out are (1) an emphasis in the last 20 years on pursuing a four-year college degree rather than working in the trades or in non degreed positions, (2) a lack of skills and tools within small businesses to effectively vet qualified candidates, and (3) an unemployment rate so low that workers are "bidding up" initial employment offers and are tempted to chase alternate offers even after they're employed.

Hiring more competent and highly paid professionals has become a direct, competitive strategy for winning more business. This is directly in line with what virtually every business expert has been writing about regarding people for the last 20 years!

The world of business has gone quantitative. Numbers are mattering more to people who care about numbers and who pay the bills. The only way small, independent business owners will be able to compete in this numbers-driven future is if they have the mainstays on board to drive down costs so they can keep their margins higher. Deeper profitability and cash flow allow companies to hire even better talent to continue the cycle of lower costs and better margins.

The days when companies could hip-shoot prices, not worry about costs, or keep sloppy records and still expect to flourish are quickly disappearing.

This doesn't mean that every large competitor is getting this right. They aren't, and that is what leaves the window of opportunity open for the small business owner who is willing to actually run their business like a business and do the hard work necessary to attract great talent.

If our people really are our biggest competitive advantage, and I truly believe they are, then the way to gain more business or to keep the business you have is by attracting and keeping the best people.

At the writing of this book, we are in a phase where there is such a scarcity of talent that businesses are forced to pay higher wages even to poor performers just to have the coverage they need to keep their doors open. The best workers are also seeking a company culture that treats people like they are key advantages, and they will only stay at a place where they feel valued.

Forging Dynasty Businesses will help small business owners recognize how the competitive landscape has shifted for workers and how it will affect their company. It then helps them focus on the adjustments they will need to go through if they want their business to thrive in the changing employment climate. And this says nothing about the legacy many business owners want to leave behind or the progeny they want to hand their company to. They may learn too late that their progeny won't want the company they're inheriting!

This book addresses the people element of a business. It doesn't touch on the financial challenges, sales and marketing challenges, digital technology challenges, or general operations challenges where sloppiness or an "I never needed that before, so why do I need it now?" attitude prevails. Those guys are walking dinosaurs who haven't been convinced to lie down yet. And while this may seem overly harsh to some people, the future may tell a different story.

Chuck Violand

Acknowledgments

While the name Chuck Violand may appear on the cover of this book, it was largely through the efforts of my colleagues at Violand Management Associates that it was written. I'd like to recognize the significant contributions of Tim Hull, Scott Tackett, John Monroe, and Bill Prosch. Their insights, case studies, and real-world experiences with our clients bring credibility to the concepts discussed.

My special thanks to Violand Management colleague Tom Cline who did the real heavy lifting with the writing. It was due to his skills as not only a writer but also as an advisor to small businesses that this book was brought to life. Additionally, his resolve to make sure the project kept moving forward was invaluable.

Great credit also goes to another of my friends and colleagues at Violand Management, Karen Tuersley. As our internal editor, Karen has a wonderful skill in taking the disjointed thoughts and mangled words we present to her and making sense of them. The message is clearer and words are more fun to read after they've passed through Karen's skillful hands.

My deep appreciation to Mike Testa and Patty Beard for their unfiltered and honest feedback. They helped make this book better.

Lastly, any acknowledgments would be incomplete without extending my deep appreciation to the hundreds of clients that Violand Management has worked with over the years and who served as a proving ground for many of the concepts discussed. It is their openness and patience that allowed this book to exist in the first place.

Introduction

After decades of working with small business owners and their teams, studying heaps of research conducted by subject matter experts and scholars, and candidly addressing the person whose face I see in the mirror every morning, the evidence is undeniable—success in business is an inside game! And your team is only as good as your people.

As noted previously, people are one of the few remaining, reliable sources of sustainable, competitive advantage. Competitors will poach your employees and copy everything you do, and technology and process advantages will fade over time, but having the best people, the right people for your organization and your mission, will turn customers into raving fans and allow you to have a more enjoyable ride as you achieve your goals.

With the rapidly shifting, competitive landscape in most industries, it's no longer just about profits; it's about survival. This supports the belief that the company with the best players wins. In fact, without great players we are left to pick up table scraps, if we're even healthy enough to still sit at the table.

Most business owners give lip service to the mantra that people are our greatest assets, but how many of us really grasp the deeper implications of this? After all, people are listed on our income statements as an expense (payroll), and they are nowhere to be found under assets on our balance sheets.

In businesses where the owner has fostered a culture in which people appear to be little more than chattel, where relationships are transactional, and where ridiculously high turnover is tolerated, what type of people do you think they will attract? How will they compete against companies with great talent and an even greater culture? Which company do you think customers are going to be attracted to and want to do business with?

Larger, more-established firms—providing they have a great reputation—are able to attract better, more-experienced workers. Not

HOW LARGER COMPANIES ATTRACT BETTER WORKERS

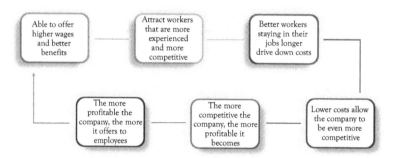

Figure I.1 Large company cycle

just entry-level or frontline workers but workers throughout the organization. They are able to pay higher wages and offer benefits that few smaller, independent firms can match. And even as they are paying those higher wages, the larger companies are still able to drive down their overall costs because their people are more experienced, more competitive, and stay in their jobs longer. The more they drive down costs, the better the company can compete, the more profitable the company becomes, and the more they can continue to offer their employees. The cycle builds on itself.

Hiring more competent and highly paid professionals to "lean out" operating costs becomes not only a path to earning more profits but a direct, competitive strategy for winning more business. What does this mean to small business owners? When we connect the dots, we can see that leaning out operating costs will allow us to attract highly talented workers. These workers may come with higher price tags, but they produce more and better work. This allows us to better compete with the larger companies while continuing to earn deeper profits.

My goal in writing this book is to help small businesses thrive in an increasingly competitive world. To provide the keys to unlock the fundamental elements of an organization that serve as the foundation for small businesses to perpetually attract and retain top talent—those who both fit with the organization's culture and core values and who contribute to achieving the organization's goals. In other words, to compete and win because they have a better team of players.

This book is written in a conversational, nonacademic style that acknowledges the trouble-shooting mindset yet short attention span and easily distracted nature of many entrepreneurs.

This is not to suggest that building a team of "A" players is easy. It's not. It requires a lot of hard work, dogged determination, and constant vigilance to ensure the team stays in top form. But it is well worth the effort, both in terms of the financial performance of the company and the joy and significant emotional rewards of working with a high-functioning team.

Forging Dynasty Businesses is not necessarily intended to be read from front to back, and the order in which the subjects are presented is not meant to imply their importance or order of operation. Instead, each chapter focuses on a particular topic or issue that my colleagues and I have found to be critical to finding, hiring, and retaining the right people. Every organization is different, as are the areas of their business in need of the most attention at any given time. The information presented for each topic is intended to assist the business owner in assessing their unique situation and applying tested remedies in the areas of need.

For additional resources, you can find the online Appendix at businessexpertpress.com, then search for Violand. This book is also a companion to the comprehensive Culture Forge™ system developed by Violand Management Associates. For more information, visit violand .com.

CHAPTER 1

Making Room for High-Performing Team Members

People are one of the few remaining, reliable sources of sustainable, competitive advantage. Competitors will copy marketing strategies, and technology and process advantages will fade over time, but having the best people, the right people for your organization and your mission, will turn customers into raving fans and allow you to have a more enjoyable journey as you achieve your goals.

The focus of the philosophy, strategies, and tools presented here is about having the right people in the right positions within your organization. This is what business author Jim Collins popularized in his book *Good to Great* when he compared business to a bus and wrote about the importance of getting the right people in the right seats. At my company, we use the term "A" players to describe those who are most desirable and who perform in ways that both support a company's culture and contribute to achieving that company's organizational goals. While "A" players are not necessarily all-stars, and they are certainly not flawless, they are the desired team members to have.

Evaluating Your Employees

Forging a dynasty team begins by assessing the employees you currently have and determining those who are capable of helping take the business where you want it to go. Executing this process is critical and requires leadership's ability to separate transactional performance from elements such as teambuilding, leadership, and behaving in ways that reinforce the core values and culture the owner has created or for which they are striving. This real-life example helps explain what we mean by transactional performance.

Deceived By Numbers

Joe has been with the company in various positions for 14 years and a project manager for the past six years. Measured by the metric of the total invoiced value of the jobs he manages, Joe is the best-performing project manager on staff. Last year, out of the total company revenue of $4.5 million, Joe managed projects totaling $1.7 million. The other three project managers on staff were all under $1 million in the projects they managed.

Although Joe's projects are normally done on time, subcontractors have reported undue pressure to get work completed, use overtime that will not be compensated, take minor shortcuts on quality that are not likely to be noticed by customers, and fit Joe's jobs into their schedule against the threat of not receiving future work if they don't.

Joe has been known to publicly berate company employees for errors or omissions in work. He invests little to no time in helping employees develop additional skills but rather threatens that they "can be replaced by someone who can" when they ask for help or guidance.

Joe's behavior is driving a series of negative effects throughout the business. Turnover is high among the people who work for Joe and those who work on the jobs he manages.

Subcontractors who are employed on Joe's jobs feel they have little choice but to put up with his tactics if they want to continue to receive work. Efforts to support the continued growth of the business by lining up additional subcontractors to take on the added volume have been hampered by Joe's reputation within the local contractor community. Despite this ripple effect, finding another project manager who can produce as much work as Joe is viewed by the owner as a challenge more painful than dealing with the occasional flare-ups that Joe ignites. The owner tolerates the negative aspects of Joe's style and behavior because "He is the most productive project manager I have."

Transactional Performance

The term *transactional* is used as it relates to certain elements of employee performance. A deeper dive into the basics of performance management will shed additional light on its meaning.

There are three key elements in managing employee performance:

1. Clearly define the responsibilities and expectations for the position, including how performance will be measured.

2. Track performance including measurements typically focused on productivity, quality, customer satisfaction, and timeliness—regardless of the area of the business or position.

3. Provide frequent, fact-based feedback to the employee including results versus expectations for the metrics defined for the position. Along with the employee, develop plans to address areas where improvement is needed.

In most cases, the metrics and expectations that are used to define performance are transactional. That is, they focus on the aspects of the employee's job that are most easily measured. Here are a few examples.

Job Title	Metrics/Measurables
Project Manager	Revenue value of jobs completed; job gross profit %
Bookkeeper	Timeliness and accuracy of entries; monthly closing on time
Estimator	Timeliness of estimates; profit margin on jobs
Sales Rep	Revenue generated; number of sales calls or meetings

These metrics reflect the objective—the measurable results or activities associated with the respective position. They are typical of models used by businesses to measure the performance of their employees and are often tied to bonus or commission structures that drive a portion of the employee's compensation. While these metrics are appropriate for the specific titles shown, they represent only a portion, the transactional side, of what should be expected in the execution of the jobs.

The performance of employees who are transactional in nature is driven solely by what will benefit them personally. If their goal is to make more money, they will focus almost exclusively on metrics that drive compensation to increase their bonus or commission. But measuring the transactional aspects of an employee's performance does not tell the entire story.

Elements of Employee Performance
That Are Non-Transactional

Let's examine other elements of employee performance, those that contribute not only to the financial or operational success of a business but also to the overall health of an organization. These include the culture, morale, and commitment level of employees, along with the ability of the total team to support sustained profitable growth.

Employee Development. Part of every manager's and supervisor's job is to help the people they manage or supervise to be successful. Training and development of employees under their responsibility contributes to improved productivity, higher employee morale, and greater retention. When employees see the organization placing a priority on helping prepare them for greater levels of responsibility and higher-paying positions, they are more engaged, their morale is higher, and they tend to be more committed. Managers or supervisors taking time to help employees learn proper procedures and new skills build their confidence and often their desire to make a career with the company, not simply hold a job that is a stepping-stone to their personal goals.

Additionally, building the bench strength that will allow the company to replace managers and other key employees who may leave the organization is an important element in succession planning. The overall capacity of the organization is expanded as a result of the commitment to employee development.

Team Player. Setting a good example by focusing on what is in the best interests of the overall organization is what being a team player is about. A company's most-experienced employees are typically sources of information and guidance for other employees, including new hires who look to those more senior for cues on what is acceptable versus what may be overlooked. A transactional employee's singular focus on getting their job done and earning the greatest possible bonus means they have little inclination to spend time helping others.

Culture. One of leadership's main responsibilities is to develop and maintain the culture of the organization. When employees are retained whose styles and behaviors are inconsistent with the core values and cultural traits of the company, others will view the inconsistency as a weakness on the owner's or leader's part. Plus, with our clients we have found that when a cultural disconnect exists between an employee and the company, it usually leads to the employee leaving the company, whether or not their departure ends up being voluntary.

Leader Support. High-performing employees who are committed to doing a good job and wish to grow and develop with an organization usually expect several things:

- Mentorship and a focus on developing their skills and abilities.

- Opportunities for advancement, with increased responsibilities and higher compensation.

- To work with other "A" players rather than being surrounded by or needing to pull extra weight for employees who don't measure up. They expect that leadership will identify and work to improve or remove low performers.

The Real Costs of Ignoring Transactional Employees

Transactional employees who focus only on what serves their personal interests and who do little to contribute to the overall health of the organization through their efforts in the areas outlined above may appear to be key players in the success of the business. In reality, they are often a root cause of high turnover and an organization's inability to retain high-level talent.

In our years of working with small businesses, we have encountered many instances where transactional employees have been part of an organization for a long time. They may have been with the owner when the business was first started and played an integral role in helping the business ramp up. They may have a personal tie to the owner that goes back many years. They often have specific skills or unique experiences that cause the owner to view them as indispensable. We've often heard comments like, "Joe is the only one who knows how to do that" or "Sue has dealt with jobs like this before, so whenever we run into this, we rely on her."

This type of situation becomes even more complicated when the transactional employees are family members. It's common for business owners to employ relatives in their company, even when those relatives don't have an equity stake in the business. It's no wonder that over 80 percent of all businesses in North America are considered to be family owned. In many cases, surrounding ourselves with people we love and trust creates a productive and pleasing work environment. But in other cases, the family aspect is mismanaged, and people are either placed in or left in positions for which they are unqualified or have little interest. Too often they remain in these positions out of loyalty to the owner or because of inflated compensation. This culture of entitlement fostered by family members breeds resentment among nonfamily workers, even if the entitlement is only perceived and not actually taking place.

When transactional or entitled employees exhibit behaviors that conflict with the core values and cultural norms of the organization, it is not uncommon for leaders or owners to respond with phrases like, "That's just Joe being Joe" or "Sue is a unique individual, but we would be lost without her." Rather than face reality with these employees and have a difficult discussion about their performance, behavior, and lack of support for the team, leadership often kicks the uncomfortable conversation down the road, making excuses for the behavior and allowing these "indispensable" employees to poison the culture of the organization.

In many of the client cases we have dealt with, here is what was occurring below the surface:

- The transactional employees were viewed by others as untouchable, although they routinely demonstrated behaviors that were not tolerated from other employees.

- Owners and leaders were viewed as weak and indecisive because they refused to deal with situations of which they were acutely aware. Their credibility became limited.

- High-performing or high-potential employees either left the organization or dialed back their level of performance to only that which was sufficient for them to be retained. They wouldn't make the extra efforts required to offset the disruption and ineffectiveness that was often caused by the transactional employees.

Make no mistake, dealing with situations like these is not easy, nor is having the uncomfortable but necessary conversations with these often long-serving employees. It's painful. The owners or managers can only think, "How am I going to replace the skills, abilities, and experience that so-and-so has?," "How are we going to make up for the revenue we'll lose when they leave?," "How can I tell my long-time friend that their behavior has turned their presence in the organization from an asset to a liability?," and when the conversation involves a family member, "What effect will this have on our next holiday dinner?"

There is an emotional attachment that business owners often have with their long-standing employees, especially those who were an integral part of the organization's start. These are the folks who worked long hours, shoulder-to-shoulder with the owner, through the perilous early years. It's hard for an owner to think about holding them accountable for behaviors they wouldn't tolerate from others. Here is an example of an owner who wouldn't.

Mission Failure

We were hired by the business owner, and one of our objectives was to help him build a management team that would support the day-to-day operations of the business without him needing to be present. There was an individual at the company, serving in an operations management position, who we intentionally did not include on the organizational chart when we presented our proposed leadership team to the owner. This individual was a transactional employee and an ineffective manager. It was our opinion that he did not have the potential to make the needed transition into a leadership role where he could become an effective member of the management team. As it turns out, he was the guy who had put in the hard work during the infancy of the business and was a close, personal friend of the owner. In the owner's mind, the business wouldn't have survived without him, so the friend was indispensable.

Our suggestion was to have us work with this individual to build up his management skills and help him gain the business acumen we

---

(*Continued*)

(*Continued*)

> felt was critical to success in his current role and to the continued success of the company.
>
> If coaching this person didn't prove to be effective, then our recommendation was to place him in another position that was a better fit for his skills and drive, thus honoring his early loyalty to the company and preserving his relationship with the owner.
>
> Unfortunately, the client didn't agree with our assessment and the owner ended up terminating our relationship.

Sometimes, in spite of our best advice, an owner may not be ready to make the changes we feel are necessary for the company to succeed.

Whether it's with the help of a trusted friend or counselor or it's on their own, when the owner or leader is ready to face the reality of what is happening within their organization, they often realize that the unseen effects of keeping transactional employees are likely more negative than the skills and abilities they were convinced they couldn't live without. Once they do, the positive results that follow inevitably convince them that the right decision was made.

The Right People in the Right Seats

Another scenario to mention, although transactional may not apply, is when a business outgrows the talents or skills of its employees. People who are effective in their job for a $500,000 or $1 million business may not be capable of handling the additional responsibilities or complexity of the same position or a similar one once the business grows into a significantly larger company. While making room for high-performing employees may not dictate that this person be removed from the organization, their best fit may be in another role for which they are better suited.

For example, an outstanding bookkeeper for a small company may not have the skills needed to fulfill the accountant/controller position as the company grows. Instead, perhaps they are better moved into an accounts payable or receivable position or an administrative support role.

Positive Change

When action is taken, either in working with an employee to change behaviors that are corrupting the culture or removing that person from the organization, the following typically happens within a relatively short period of time.

1. Some employees communicate to the owner that they are glad the issue was addressed and changes were made. This communication may include comments along the lines of, "What took you so long?"

2. Employees who had previously been holding back or who had been evaluated as average performers suddenly blossom and become more highly engaged, productive, and valuable.

   Think about the situation with Joe, the project manager. There were other project managers in the organization who weren't producing as much revenue as Joe. It's possible that the output of one or more of the people already on the payroll could be increased by investing in additional training, development, and coaching.

3. Others will step forward to pick up whatever slack exists in cases where the transactional employee is no longer with the organization.

4. The owner feels a huge sense of relief! The burden that was felt (if only subconsciously) to deal with the behavior, and the knowledge that they had the responsibility to take action, is finally lifted.

A rule of thumb we suggest our clients use to determine their gut feeling about whether to remove an employee is to ask themselves how they'd feel if that employee turned in their resignation. Would they be anxious or would they be relieved? The answer to this question usually helps them make their decision.

When business owners fail to make the difficult but critical decision to retain only those employees who perform at a high level and are a good fit with the cultural values, mission, and vision of the organization, a couple of things happen. First, they risk losing the "A" players they already have. Second, they miss creating opportunities to upgrade their organization by replacing those who may be performing transactionally and, as a result, are holding back the business in other ways.

Effective leaders recognize these negative effects and allow the Joes and Sues of the world to flourish in roles better suited for their talents, making room for those who are a good fit with the organization's culture and will contribute to achieving the organization's goals.

CHAPTER 2

Career Path Development for Your People

One of the most critical requirements for attracting, hiring, and retaining "A" players is the ability to show them the potential for a long career with adequate opportunities for personal, professional, and financial growth. The owner and leaders of your organization must be committed to this long-term strategy. Many elements to effectively executing this philosophy are covered in this chapter.

Advancement From Entry-Level Positions

While some candidates may be hesitant to even accept an entry-level position, if they do, a requirement for keeping them on board is that they see two things:

1. A path of positions with increasing responsibilities.

2. Evidence of people who have started at the entry level and worked their way to positions of greater responsibility and increased compensation.

In large businesses, it's common for managers and executives to be motivated by "climbing the corporate ladder." In small businesses, the ladder is still there, but there usually aren't as many rungs to climb before bumping up against the owner. This is what we refer to as "The Short Ladder"; a situation that can present challenges for small business owners who want to retain talented workers. Most competent people want to grow professionally, be part of a successful team, and see their company succeed. It's this professional growth and feeling that you are part of a winning team that brings meaning and excitement to a job.

In a company that has stopped growing, or when an owner stops developing themselves professionally, an already short ladder is shortened even more, creating additional challenges for attracting and keeping talented people. This is one of many reasons it is so critical for business owners to continue to develop themselves as business leaders.

When talented employees find themselves stuck on The Short Ladder behind an owner who is unable or unwilling to either lead the company forward or move aside, they start questioning their own future. Career-oriented people seek opportunities to exercise their talents and test their skills. If their current workplace fails to provide this, they will be drawn to companies that do.

At the same time, it would be a mistake to assume that all employees want to climb the corporate ladder or take on management responsibilities. Many are satisfied with continuing to grow in their current position by refining their skills through professional development. This is especially true with the younger generations who want work–life balance. They don't want to "work their lives away" like their parents. It's a work-to-live view versus the live-to-work view that many of us old-timers grew up with.

Positional Ladders

For those hired into technical positions that deliver services to customers, such as technicians or service professionals, there should be a ladder that can be climbed or a succession of titles, positions, or responsibilities that don't require moving into a supervisory role. The ladder should reflect a series of positions and corresponding compensation increases that are based primarily on different types and levels of technical skills and responsibilities. Consider this a "pay for performance" model where those employees who can perform more or different types of work, or deliver more or different types of services, are more valuable to the organization and, therefore, are more highly compensated.

This ladder philosophy can apply to any department or function within an organization. While it is most often used for positions in operations, it is appropriate anywhere there are a sufficient number of employees and varying levels of capabilities. For example, if the business involves a group of customer service employees who communicate remotely with prospects and customers, there may be three or four levels of representatives who deal with progressively more-complex customer problems or who have increasing levels of authority to provide on-the-spot remedies to customer complaints. The same can be said for multiple employees in a company's finance or business development departments.

The following steps can serve as a guide in creating this positional ladder and accompanying wage scale.

1. Document the hourly pay rate for the most fundamental position(s) in the department.

2. Determine the highest rate of hourly pay for positions that are just below the supervisor level.

3. Insert the job title(s) for entry-level positions and define the skills or capabilities expected from employees in these positions.

4. List the title and skills/capabilities that represent the next level up on the position ladder.

5. Repeat this process until all appropriate positions, titles, and capabilities have been documented.

6. Determine the starting hourly pay rates for each position on the ladder.

Once this information has been completed for each department in which it is applicable, you will have written documentation of the career ladder that is available to employees whose growth path may not include supervisory roles.

Promoting From Within

An important aspect of the long-term career philosophy is the idea that open positions will be filled by people within the company, whenever possible. This reinforces the concept of providing opportunities to employees who prove themselves and strive to grow professionally through training and development. Benefits to the organization, in addition to higher morale and lower employee turnover, include the fact that you already know the employee. You understand their strengths and weaknesses, along with areas where development will be needed to improve their likelihood of success in the new role. Likewise, these internal employees already understand your culture and know the people with whom they will be working.

A word of caution: as mentioned above, not all employees are motivated by corporate advancement. Many are not hardwired for or motivated by management positions. In these cases, the notion of rewarding a loyal, hardworking employee with increased responsibility isn't a reward at all. Instead, it serves to demotivate a previously motivated worker.

Promoting from within doesn't mean you won't ever hire people from the outside. Situations will arise where the needed skills and experience don't exist within the organization or the need for new technologies, ideas, and perspectives require hiring as opposed to promoting from within.

Organizational Chart

An organizational chart provides a visual image of the positions and hierarchy within a company and helps employees to see the career advancement paths that are available. On the next page is a sample organizational chart.

As a business grows and new services are added, the positions and job titles within the organization change. The organizational chart should be updated regularly to reflect changes in areas such as:

- Positions and titles within the business

- Names of individuals holding each position

- The hierarchy or reporting structure (who reports to whom)

As employees join the company and advance in their skills and abilities, they are able to see the overall structure of the organization and positions to which they may aspire.

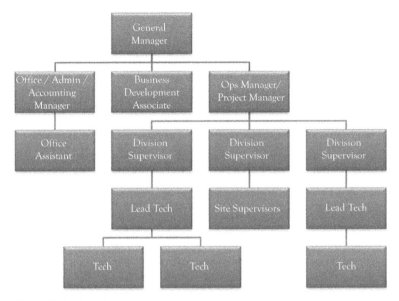

Figure 2.1 Org chart

Updating the Organizational Chart

Here are some additional things to look for in order to be sure your organizational charts are as up to date as possible.

- Note any changes to position titles or names of people holding specific jobs. Include additions that occurred due to increased business volume (e.g., added another Business Development Associate or Project Manager).

- Verify that the chain of command shown is accurate.

- Identify any positions that are currently unfilled and note as such.

- Include future roles that will need to be filled in the next few months.

- If new positions have been created and recruiting is underway, show the title in the appropriate area of the chart.

Commitment to Training and Development

Beyond technical skills and knowledge, training plans should be in place for every position within the business. Every employee who moves or is hired into a new position should have a defined training program. The length of the training period will likely vary by position.

Development is different from training. Development refers to employees being encouraged and given opportunities to take on new and increased responsibilities, being coached and mentored by those with greater experience, and being regularly involved in discussions about their goals and aspirations.

Employee development involves two key aspects.

1. Help employees to improve performance in their current role.

2. Prepare employees for positions of greater responsibility.

Refer to Chapter 11 on Professional Development for additional information on technical training and employee development.

Performance Management

Successful career paths are those where the individual reaches their full potential. As mentioned earlier, effective managers realize that not every employee has the ability or desire to become a manager or department head. In addition to consistently tracking and providing feedback on individual performance, managers should also provide employees with objective assessments combined with one-on-one discussions to help guide career planning and employee development.

To be successful, managers need to be capable of the following.

- Assess employee performance, skills, strengths, and weaknesses without bias.

- Regularly communicate with employees regarding their performance and where improvement is needed.

- Provide positive reinforcement and feedback whenever employees are caught doing something correctly or well.

- Develop plans with individual employees for the improvement of their skills and knowledge.

- Track the execution of development plans and changes in employee performance.

To learn more about Performance Management, visit Chapter 8.

Tracking Performance

It is important to be able to track performance to measure the impact of changes you have made that are pertinent to the subject of career paths. When using these or other key performance indicators to track performance improvement, be sure to measure your current performance, perhaps going back in time a year or two, to set a baseline. Then track the same metrics after you implement your changes to verify that you are achieving the intended results.

In your annual business planning process, include setting targets or goals for the coming year for the chosen metrics. Here are some examples:

Promotions—number of employees promoted out of entry-level positions over the past 12 months.

Management Position Fill Rate—percent of supervisory or management position openings that have been filled by promoting existing employees during the past 12 months.

Performance Rating Participation Rate—number of employees given a specific score or rating on their performance evaluation divided by the total number of employees.

Training/Development Hours—sum of total training hours for all employees divided by the total number of employees.

CHAPTER 3

Company Culture

A company's ability to attract and retain top-level talent is based, in part, on the culture within the organization and the resulting reputation with the marketplace. Explaining the organization's mission, vision, and core values to job applicants and focusing on candidates who appear to be a good fit with the company's culture are critical elements of the hiring process.

A company's culture reflects the values and style of the business owner or CEO. Owners must understand that any inconsistency in the company's stated values and cultural traits versus actual behaviors, demeanor, and policies will result in an environment where people respond and behave based on what they see and hear from their leaders—not on what is written in the mission or vision statements. High-performing employees will likely choose to leave if the actual culture is not as advertised. To put it another way, it's not the talk the owner talks. It's the walk the owner walks. Here is a tale of two cultures to articulate this point.

A Tale of Two Cultures

As you might imagine, during the course of working with hundreds of companies we have encountered a wide spectrum of business owners—a wide range in the levels of energy, ego, intelligence, formal education, business experience, and vision for where they wanted to take their business. With culture reflecting the style, demeanor, and leadership philosophy of the owner, our experience has revealed an oft-repeated pattern of two extremes.

Culture #1

This is a stagnated business that has been limping along for years, being marginally profitable. Revenue has plateaued in a narrow

---

(Continued)

(Continued)

range. Employee turnover is relatively high, and the level of employee engagement is low. In most cases, there are mediocre players in key positions. The culture in this organization is not attractive to high-performing individuals.

In a company like this, being the smartest person in the room is a driver for the owner. Their ego is inflated and needs constant feeding. There is no desire to recognize their own personal areas of weakness and address them either through personal development or by hiring people with complementary strengths. Those in management roles have limited authority and, therefore, limited interest in challenging or pushing back against the owner in an effort to effect change.

This egocentric owner is prone to lashing out at times, whether to employees, customers, or strategic partners. Voices are raised, inappropriate things are said, and participants are left feeling hurt and reminded that change is unlikely. Rather than taking a personal interest in their people, this owner flaunts their own lifestyle, continually posting photos of their unique and exciting experiences on social media and, in extreme cases, using the company's warehouse to store their expensive toys in the off-season, constantly reminding employees of the difference in their "station in life." High-potential employees, if they exist, are quick to head for the exit.

Culture #2

This business is a breath of fresh air. Capable managers are in place and represent a leadership team that often manages the business on a day-to-day basis without significant participation by the owner. Employees understand the business goals, what success looks like, what is expected of them, and how performance is measured. They are given the tools to be successful and there is a focus on continually investing in the development of people. Roles and responsibilities are clear. Employees are empowered. When questions arise or decisions are needed, they tend to happen at a level in the organization much closer to the customer, as decisions are frequently delegated to those below management positions.

Contrary to the first scenario, this owner recognizes that they are neither the smartest one in the room nor do they need to be. They want to find people who are smarter, more experienced, and better equipped than they are to help grow the business and the people within the organization. This owner does not feel threatened by someone who is more capable.

Employees in this culture are more engaged. They know their ideas count. People ask for their input and leaders listen. There are opportunities for growth because the business is growing. Business planning is a team process where departments are challenged with how they can continually improve and contribute to reaching the organization's goals. Problems are addressed, not by figuring out who is to blame but by identifying the root cause(s) and taking steps to eliminate them and prevent the problem from recurring.

Importantly, not all owners whose business cultures are described positively started out that way. Many we have encountered are second-generation owners who have a different vision for the business than their parents had and a different perspective on their role. These owners often face the challenge of others perceiving that they were handed the business and aren't likely interested in working hard to maintain or grow it.

Those with the right mindset continually talk with their people, are visible on job sites, and have a true interest in getting to know and staying in touch with their employees. They work hard to earn people's respect and to communicate where the business is going. They prove themselves. High performers look to these owners for career opportunities and to pursue their own personal and professional growth.

Owner Accountability for Culture

As mentioned above, the culture of any organization is defined more by how the CEO or senior leaders behave than by what they say. Hanging the company's mission or core values in highly visible locations throughout the company can serve as either a source of inspiration or can be a source of cynicism to the rest of the company if leaders aren't acting in alignment with what's hanging on the wall.

The culture of a company can be more accurately defined as how people feel at work. Not just the values they believe in, but more importantly how they live those values through interactions with their co-workers, customers, suppliers, and even people in their communities. How employees feel about the culture is demonstrated in where they see the company going and what they're doing to help get it there. In a nutshell, a description of a company's culture is a shared set of values, goals, attitudes, and practices that make up an organization.

Indicators of the owner or CEO's focus on culture include:

- How often they recognize and praise individual employees for demonstrating the core values and interacting with others in ways that reinforce the company's culture

- The extent of their focus on company culture and assessing a candidate's likely fit as part of the hiring process

- Participation by the owner in the new-hire onboarding process, with a focus on explaining and reinforcing the company's culture, mission, vision, and core values

- The number of occasions when culture, teamwork, and core values are included on agendas for employee meetings or for the leadership team

- The owner maintaining behavioral cohesion by frequently clarifying the mission and vision of the organization

The Role of Management

A healthy organizational culture includes clarity on what every person's job is, what they are expected to do and accomplish, how their performance will be evaluated, and what authority they have to make decisions and allocate resources. Everyone in a management position should be accountable for ensuring this clarity exists for all employees who fall under their leadership.

Like the business owner or CEO, management's behavior, decision making, and priorities should reflect and reinforce the organization's core values. Recognizing people who behave in ways that display those values should be a regular occurrence. Leaders cannot simply talk about the company culture; they must live it.

Managers should constantly be monitoring employee morale, reinforcing behaviors that display core values, and soliciting feedback on levels of teamwork, satisfaction, and cooperation.

Mission, Vision, and Core Values

Priorities, decisions made, and treatment of employees and stakeholders should always reflect a company's mission, vision, and core values.

- An organization's mission statement provides its reason for existence. It answers the question "Why do we exist or do what we do?"

- The vision statement is a description of what the organization will be or have accomplished at a point 7 to 10 years in the future once the current goals have been achieved. It answers the question "Where are we going?"

- A company's core values describe its personality or its heart. These values, typically four to six, explain what is most important to the organization for how everyone works together, treats and communicates with each other and customers, and how decisions are made.

The content of these statements and values should be consistently demonstrated every day by leaders and employees alike. Owners and managers should make a habit of reinforcing the statements and values in meetings, in discussions with employees, and as part of the interviewing and onboarding processes.

Accountability

High-performing employees want to be held accountable for their performance. All employees, from the owner down, should be held accountable.

There should be no exceptions made for family members, long-time employees, or those otherwise perceived as vital to the business based on their possession of specific skills or experiences.

Phrases like the following, when used to explain or excuse behavior, are clear signs that there are inconsistencies in accountability, which will undermine an organization's culture.

"That's just Joe being Joe."

"We can't get rid of Sue, she's the only one who knows how to _____."

"He's the owner's nephew, although no one is really sure what his job is."

"Bob has been around forever. He's a high school buddy of the owner."

"I can't get rid of her. She's been with me from the beginning."

Performance Management

Formal and consistent processes should be in place for assessing the performance of all employees and communicating with them regarding their strengths and where improvement is needed. All managers should be trained in performance management and should conduct effective performance reviews. This is covered in more detail in Chapter 8, dedicated to Performance Management.

Training and Employee Development

The performance management process should include a definition of skills and the knowledge areas where improvement is needed. Coming to an agreement with the individual employee on specific areas of focus should then lead to establishing a documented plan for how those needs will be addressed and who is responsible for making that happen.

All those within the organization who have management responsibilities must understand that the continued development of the individuals for whom they are responsible is an important aspect of their job. Reluctance to train and develop people, because the manager views it as a potential threat to their position and power, is a clear sign of an unhealthy culture.

Employee development includes not only dealing with areas where improvement in skills or knowledge is needed for the current position but also looking to prepare employees for positions of greater responsibility in support of succession planning and company growth.

You can find more information on Professional Development in Chapter 11.

Teamwork

Organizations often include teamwork as a core value. While it is viewed as a desirable element in a company's culture, lip service is as far as many companies go when it comes to teamwork and how work is actually done, how decisions are made, and how people communicate and treat each other. Effective teamwork is built on trust, open and honest communication, and mutual resolution of disagreements.

Effective teamwork displays the following characteristics:

- The organization has created clear expectations for the team's work, and the team is committed to achieving them.

- Team members trust each other and are comfortable taking reasonable risks when it comes to disagreements, communication, and decision making.

- Communication is open, honest, and respectful.

- Team members admit weaknesses and mistakes, and no one is afraid to ask for help.

- There is a strong sense of group commitment. Differing backgrounds and experiences are viewed as assets to the team.

- Creativity, innovation, and different viewpoints are expected and encouraged.

- Teams engage in continuous improvement in the ways they interact and work together.

- Members work toward mutual resolution of problems and disagreements.

- Multiple participants contribute to leading the team.

- The team makes high-quality decisions together and has the support and commitment of the group to carry out the decisions made.

- Conflict among team members is viewed as healthy and is never personal.

- Team members have each other's back when someone is struggling.

Culture and Trust

Business owners, general managers, and executives are often not privy to discussions that take place among employees regarding their issues, complaints, levels of satisfaction, and bosses. This "chirping" happens when employees either don't feel comfortable taking their issues to management or they have tried that route and gotten no satisfaction. Worse yet is if they were berated for bringing up issues.

Employee "chirping" is a sign of an unhealthy culture—more specifically, one where employees feel that management does not have their best interests at heart. Typically, this type of culture is driven by a strong focus on short-term results and performance rather than a longer view rooted in ensuring that employees (and customers) remain inspired to continue contributing.

A long-term approach welcomes the disruption of change and the challenge to be transformed by it, with leaders asking their people to help them figure out how to move toward a more limitless vision of the future. But this doesn't happen without trust.

For trust to develop, employees—and managers on a leadership team, for that matter—must feel safe to express themselves. They must feel safe feeling vulnerable. Asking for help is an example of expressing vulnerability. When someone asks for help in an organization with a culture of trust, they do so with the confidence that their boss or co-workers will be there to support them. When employees feel this level of trust and consistently see it in action, they are much more likely to take issues that would otherwise result in "chirping" to their boss, the owner, or someone in a position of leadership.

Tracking Performance

It is important to be able to track performance to measure the impact of changes you have made that are pertinent to the subject of company culture. When using these or other key performance indicators to track performance improvement, be sure to measure your current performance, perhaps going back in time a year or two, to set a baseline. Then track the same metrics after you implement your changes to verify that you are achieving the intended results.

In your annual business planning process, include setting targets or goals for the coming year for the chosen metrics. Here are some examples:

Owner Onboarding—total number of hours the business owner or CEO invested in new employee onboarding over the past year.

Training/Development Hours—sum of total training hours for all employees during the past year divided by the number of employees.

Performance Metric Achievement—number of key performance indicators where goals were met or exceeded divided by the total number of performance goals. This can be measured monthly, quarterly, or annually depending on the metrics.

Suggestion Implementation—number of employee suggestions or improvement ideas that are implemented divided by the total number of suggestions received.

Tenure—average number of years of service at the organization across all employees.

CHAPTER 4

Compensation

When dealing with employee compensation in any organization, it is important to understand its role and limitations. Contrary to what many believe, compensation is not typically a sustainable source of motivation. While many qualified compensation experts have opinions on the role compensation plays in motivating workers, we have found that increases in compensation often boost employee motivation or engagement, but the effects are usually temporary.

Philosophy

Based on many studies of employee behavior and motivation, compensation is best thought of like the ante in a game of poker—it's the cost to be in the game. For employees, this means that when the appropriate level of compensation (from the employee's perspective) is not present, it is viewed as a negative. It detracts from their level of satisfaction and becomes a source of dissatisfaction with the job. When compensation is viewed as fair and adequate, it is not a strong driver or motivator. It is simply seen as one of the elements required for a position to be considered a good job. Only in the absence of what is deemed fair pay does it become a strong influence and that is as a negative.

Given the above, it is the responsibility of the business owner(s) and executives to determine where their employee compensation levels will be, relative to the market and competition. This is called "pay level." For example, to attract and retain the absolute best employees in the market or to increase the likelihood that you will continue to attract a high number of applicants during times of low unemployment, you could decide to pay 10 percent above market levels of compensation for all positions. This is a strategic or cultural decision that will drive the assessment process described below. Note that this concept of pay level is different from "pay structure," which is a set of decisions on how to price (compensate) different jobs within the organization.

When Generosity Meets Financial Reality

When it comes to compensation, an owner's desire to do right by their people, either to get them to join the company or to keep them on board, can lead to a multitude of problems. This can also be caused by the owner simply not being aware of what comparable positions pay in other companies. Good intentions must be tempered by consistency, simplicity, and budget consciousness. Here's a glimpse into our experience.

Differing Compensation Philosophies

On one end of the spectrum lies the owner whose decisions on compensation are driven by fear of not being able to hire the right people or of losing those they have. Requests for increased pay or unique bonus or commission models, whether for those already on board or for candidates to hire, are almost always granted.

One result of compensation being driven by fear is wage inflation—the condition where most positions are overcompensated when compared to the local labor market. What is affordable is not a consideration when giving in to employee demands. In extreme cases, this leads to a detrimental impact on profitability that can sink the company.

The second effect of this philosophy is complexity. With myriad compensation and incentive models based on different metrics and performance expectations, the time and cost required to collect data, track performance, and calculate pay and incentives become unrealistic.

As you might imagine, compensation can become even more complicated when family is involved in a business. Oftentimes, in a misplaced effort to take care of family members, the owner inflates their compensation, even for entry-level positions, or provides them with perks that are not available to other employees.

In many of the situations at this end of the spectrum, the free-for-all compensation philosophy becomes a discouragement for employees rather than a motivator. Performance expectations aren't clear and the key performance indicator goals that drive incentive payouts are misunderstood or not appropriate for the position. The result is poor morale. Employees feel as though they've been misled or cheated. The cycle continues when employees who complain about inadequate bonuses or commissions are mollified with additional payments. Employees soon find out that there aren't resources available to do the things needed to operate the business effectively.

The other end of the compensation philosophy continuum is fairness, consistency, and realistic cost control. Understanding the market value of the positions within the business forms the basis for establishing realistic pay ranges. Conscious decisions are made about compensation levels, taking into consideration both budget constraints and where the company's pay rates fall relative to the local labor market and the competition.

Incentive compensation plans are used sparingly and only where the position has total or significant control over the performance measures that drive that bonus or commission. Target levels of performance—those that must be met for the incentive to kick in— are built into the annual business plan and are clearly communicated to all affected team members. Incentive calculations are simple and can be performed by employees throughout the period. All employees with the same title are compensated under the same model. Increases in hourly pay rates or salary levels are driven either by an individual employee's expanded skills and capabilities or by demonstrated improvements in performance as measured by agreed-upon metrics.

The result is employees who believe they are treated fairly and consistently. They understand how they are paid and how they can increase their compensation over time. Morale tends to be higher, and team members focus on the areas and metrics they can control that will contribute to the overall success of the business.

People costs are the single largest budget item for any labor-driven service business. They must be planned and budgeted consistently. This isn't to say that people are a cost to be managed. Rather, they are an investment to be tracked. Receiving an appropriate return on that investment is driven by having the right people, continually training and developing them, and focusing all team members on the metrics that will keep the business growing while maintaining or improving profitability.

Market Assessment

A company's ability to attract and retain top-level talent is based, in part, on the level and content of compensation and employee benefits relative to other employers who are competing for the same resources. There are two distinct elements required to effectively manage employee compensation:

1. Knowing what the market and your competition are providing

2. Determining where you want your company to be positioned relative to the market and your direct competitors

Assessing the labor market and competitor practices should be reviewed annually as part of the business planning process. Changes that are implemented and the resulting budget requirements should be included in the financial forecast for the upcoming year. Data and information on compensation being provided by other employers in the market can be derived from multiple sources, such as:

- Published government data such as state, county, or local statistics

- Business organizations, local Chamber of Commerce, and human resource organizations such as the Society for Human Resource Management (SHRM)

- Violand Management Associates annual compensation survey (for consulting clients)

- Exit interview content from employees who leave the company

- Feedback provided by people who join the company

Assessments and comparisons should differentiate between exempt and nonexempt employees.

Market Compensation Assessment

Conducting a market compensation assessment consists of completing the following steps:

1. Create a list of position titles within your organization and determine which are exempt and which are nonexempt.

2. List the direct competitors in your market area that you feel are targeting the same quality of candidates as your company.

3. List other service industries that are recruiting for similar positions and their employee characteristics.

4. Research and collect data on compensation levels, by position, for comparable industries and specific competitors in your market area.

5. Compare market compensation levels with those in your company, by position, and identify where your current compensation levels fall.

6. Note positions where the data shows discrepancies between your company's compensation and the pay level you established (see section on Philosophy above).

Total Compensation

When performing any comparisons of compensation for specific positions, it is critical to include all elements of the compensation package. The specific elements will vary from position to position but can include:

- Base pay, whether hourly rate or salary

- Overtime

- Position-specific bonuses, commissions, or incentives

- Broad-based or companywide bonuses based on company performance, like profit sharing

A related issue is that of market perception. Total compensation that consists of a given hourly rate, for example, plus a bonus model based on jobs completed, estimates written, projected gross profit, or other appropriate key performance indicators may result in projected annual pay that is at least equal to a salary or higher flat-hourly rate. We've experienced situations where candidates have turned down job offers or existing employees were unhappy with bonus or commission structures because they wanted a simple hourly rate where they felt more comfortable projecting their earnings. Despite the fact that there was more upside potential in the pay with bonus structure, the known hourly rate was the preferred model within the local labor market.

Changes to Incentives, Pay Plans, and Bonuses

Changes in external markets and internal business conditions will drive the need for adjustments to company compensation, incentive, and bonus plans. These changes must be thoroughly analyzed and the results included in the annual financial forecast by using the following steps:

1. Calculate the impact of changes in hourly pay rates and salary levels and include them in monthly financial projections for the appropriate cost categories. Consider the timing of compensation changes when projecting monthly costs.

2. Project costs for all existing and updated incentive and bonus plans based on projected revenues and profits for the coming year. Include them in the appropriate lines of the financial forecast.

Budgeting and Business Planning

Financial costs associated with all employee compensation should be included in the annual budget or financial forecast that is created as part of the business planning process. Cost projections should be developed for each position and include input or assumptions on the following:

- **Amount of overtime**

- **Revenue level**

- **Revenue mix**—the percentage of total revenue that will come from each type of service or product

- **Gross profit performance**—this is reflected in both the financial proforma at the cost of goods sold level and in compensation or bonus payouts for those where the incentive is based on gross profits

- **Sales or business development commissions**—based on the commission structure(s) in place and the assumptions about where business will come from

- **Profit sharing**—if such a program is in place, what the projected payout will be based on the forecasted financial performance

Actual costs should be compared to budget figures on a quarterly basis. Variances should be analyzed, discrepancies resolved, and adjustments made to future budget periods as needed.

Effective Incentive Pay Plans

Statistics show that a relatively low percentage of organizations with incentive compensation plans in place find that the plans have a direct impact on their ability to achieve their business objectives. This lack of a direct link between incentive compensation and achievement of overall business objectives should be an important consideration for all incentive or bonus plans. The point is not that incentive compensation is ineffective but recognizing that it is not a quick fix that will result in turning around business performance.

Here are the five keys to a successful incentive plan.

1. **Simplicity**—Do the people who are affected by it understand it? Can it be explained during an elevator ride? Can the employees calculate their own bonus based on the information given to them?

2. **Clear goals**—Are the goals clear? Are they fully supported by ownership and management?

3. **Realistic goals**—Are the goals neither too difficult nor too easy to achieve?

4. **Consistency**—Is the plan aligned with the organization's present goals? Company goals change over time, so there are few organizations that have the same business objectives for five to seven years.

5. **Regular communication**—Does management regularly communicate with employees about the plan? Can they see their performance and the impact it has on the incentive?

Communication is critical. If employees don't know how they're doing, the incentive is ineffective. Information needed to calculate the individual's payout must be provided to them.

Visual communication is most effective. People want a scorecard, so show them what the actual results are and what the goals are. Ensure they understand the relationship between performance and incentive—what it means to them. This gets back to the first item, simplicity. Employees need to be able to make the connection to know what the impact will be on their compensation. If there are complex formulas and multiple contingencies involved, they will become frustrated and give up.

Tracking Performance

It is important to be able to track performance to measure the impact of changes you have made that are pertinent to the subject of compensation. When using these or other key performance indicators to track performance improvement, be sure to measure your current performance, perhaps going back in time a year or two, to set a baseline. Then track the same metrics after you implement your changes to verify that you are achieving the intended results.

In your annual business planning process, include setting targets or goals for the coming year for the chosen metrics. Here are some examples:

Direct Labor Cost—direct labor cost as a percentage of total revenue.

Total Labor Cost—total of all compensation for people in the organization as a percentage of total revenue.

At-Risk Compensation—percentage of total compensation that is derived from bonus or incentive plans.

Compensation Position—compensation level for a specific position (title) as a percentage of the mean external market compensation level.

CHAPTER 5

Employee Benefits

A company's ability to attract and retain top-level talent is based, in part, on the level and content of compensation and employee benefits relative to other employers who are competing for the same resources (people).

There are two distinct elements required to effectively manage employee benefits:

1. Knowing what the market and the competition are providing

2. Determining where you want your company to be positioned relative to the market and your direct competitors

Labor Market Assessment

Conducting an assessment of your labor market and competitor practices should be done annually and reviewed as part of the business planning process. Changes that are implemented, along with the resulting budget requirements, should be included in the financial forecast for the upcoming year. Data and information on benefits being provided by other employers in the labor market can be derived from multiple sources, such as:

- Published government data, such as state, county, or local statistics

- Business organizations, local Chamber of Commerce, and human resource organizations such as the Society for Human Resource Management (SHRM)

- Violand Management Associates annual compensation survey (for consulting clients)

- Exit interview content from employees who leave your company

- Feedback provided by people who join your company

Where possible, assessments and comparisons should differentiate between exempt and nonexempt employees.

For the most updated sample list of employer-provided benefit categories, visit the SHRM website at shrm.org.

Market Assessment

The annual assessment process should include documenting updated information regarding the benefits offered by your company and those offered by the organizations with whom you are competing for employees. For the initial assessment, begin by listing the benefits you currently offer. As you gather information on direct competitors and others in your labor market, note any additional benefits on your list, along with the organizations providing them.

Using the market information, determine where you want your company to be positioned. Then determine what changes are needed to the benefits you are currently offering.

Additional research will be required to estimate the annual cost of proposed changes and integrate them into your financial forecast. Decisions can then be made as to the nature and timing of any changes to your existing employee benefits.

Your annual planning process should include updating the benefits information for your company and those you are tracking in your labor market. Proposed changes should be evaluated as far as what the employees want and what the company can afford. The estimated costs of changes you decide to implement should be included in your business plan.

Be sure to investigate and include additional no- or low-cost benefits through policy changes pertaining to areas such as work schedules; paid time off including vacation, holidays, sick leave, and so on; break room beverages and snacks; etc.

Government Laws and Regulations

Your annual market assessment should include any updates from federal, state, and local laws or regulation changes that impact those benefits required to be provided by employers. Recognize that state or local governments may implement laws containing requirements, or that apply to organizations with different numbers of employees, than outlined in federal statutes.

Information on these changes, including effective dates, applicable organization size, and sources for additional information, can be sourced from:

- Recognized human resource organizations (SHRM)

- Business organizations (Chambers of Commerce)

- Attorneys and consultants specializing in labor and employment law

Budgeting and Cost Analysis

Financial costs associated with employee benefits should be included in the annual budget or financial forecast that is created as part of your business planning process. Cost projections should be created for each benefit type and include information or assumptions on per-person costs and the anticipated level of employee participation. Input from vendors should be included for items such as health care, outsourced training, continuing education, professional certifications, and employee clothing or tools.

Actual costs should ideally be compared to budget figures monthly, but no less often than quarterly. Variances should be analyzed, discrepancies resolved, and adjustments made to future budget periods as needed.

Training and Education

Periodic training should be used to provide added value to employees for benefits that are offered by the company and to ensure that employees understand and take advantage of all resources available to them. Vendors should be leveraged to provide regular in-house training on items like health care, insurance coverage, 401(k) investment options, and payroll deductions. The next best option is to make employees aware of available open-training sessions or online resources.

Arranging for professionals to conduct in-house, company-specific training for employees on topics like personal finances, managing credit, investment options, and budgeting are benefits that may provide significant worth, serving to reinforce your company's core values while being available at a relatively low cost.

Non-Job-Related Training

Offering employees training or education on topics that are not directly related to their jobs, but which may provide value to them in personal growth and peace of mind, can be a low-cost means of increasing morale, building loyalty, and differentiating your company in the eyes of potential employees. You might begin by examining participation rates in benefit programs you already offer. Where participation is low, work with the providers to arrange for ways to share additional information about how your people could be receiving more value.

There will undoubtedly be people available in your area who can provide education in life skills such as budgeting and financial planning, funding a college education, healthy eating and meal planning, and the availability of social service organizations and resources. You might begin by soliciting feedback from employees on proposed topics and then investigating available resources and costs.

Tracking Performance

It is important to be able to track performance to measure the impact of changes you have made that are pertinent to the subject of employee benefits. When using these or other key performance indicators to track performance improvement, be sure to measure your current performance, perhaps going back in time a year or two, to set a baseline. Then track the same metrics after you implement your changes to verify that you are achieving the intended results.

In your annual business planning process, include setting targets or goals for the coming year for the chosen metrics. Here are some examples:

Benefits Training—sum of all non-job-related or benefits training hours provided.

Turnover (annual)—number of employees who left the organization during the past year as a percentage of the total year-end employee count.

Benefit or Program Cost Per Employee—total cost of an employee benefit or program divided by the total number of employees.

Benefits/Salary Ratio—annual benefits cost divided by annual salary.

CHAPTER 6

Onboarding

Onboarding is about welcoming new employees into your company culture and getting them up to speed so they can be productive as quickly as possible. Effective onboarding of new team members can drive productivity, accelerate learning, and improve talent retention.

Traditionally, onboarding has been treated as a one- or two-day orientation event rather than a process. New hires were passive participants where they received information on employee policies and procedures, signed lots of paperwork, and were (perhaps) given a tour and introduced to other employees.

It is now recognized that the first few weeks and months are a critical period in the employee life cycle because this period lays the foundation for future success. Enlightened organizations plan for all new hires to be set up for success right from the start by making sure they have the tools, resources, and information they need.

Supporting the Culture and Business Growth

Companies that are growing and adding new employees are at risk of losing what makes them exceptional. You need to be intentional about what makes you excellent and diligent about passing that on to everyone who joins your team. Typically, this consists of the systems, processes, and culture that define who you are, how you deliver your products and services, and how you treat your customers.

Introducing new team members to the elements that make the company different and immersing them into the culture early on generates commitment to your key elements and values.

Yet, despite the importance of setting the stage at the outset for a positive employment experience, few companies handle it correctly by assigning ownership and having a process. Instead, they take a learn-on-the-fly approach to onboarding and hope it turns out okay. The following experiences illustrate this point.

Onboarding: What Not to Do

Early in my career, I was working with a construction company to develop orientation and training guidelines. I was meeting with several of the company's foremen and field supervisors when the conversation turned to their initial experiences with the company. Without exception, they all shared the fear, isolation, and confusion they experienced on the morning of their first day. These were burly guys not given to expressing their emotions. Yet, here they were, emotionally relating how they had no idea who they were supposed to meet, where they were supposed to be, or what they were supposed to do. One talked about standing next to a wall to avoid getting run over as the trucks and equipment were being driven out of the yard.

The guys I was meeting with had been with the company for years, so clearly things had improved significantly since their first days. This was largely due to the owner who had developed into a very effective business leader. But it doesn't always turn out so well as is demonstrated in this next example.

We had just started working with this client when they shared the story about a new hire who lasted only three days. On the third day, the owner had a nonmedical, family emergency he needed to attend to, so he handed the new hire some brochures and told him to go out and make sales calls. No instructions were given about who to call on or what to say. Interestingly enough, this was an employee hired for production work and not for sales. I can only imagine what he was thinking!

Before the owner had even returned to the office, the new hire texted to let him know "the job isn't for me" and resigned.

The last example above would be funny if it were an isolated event at one company. Unfortunately, we see this scenario play out in different ways far more often than you can imagine.

Onboarding

How new employees feel about their first few days at a company will have a huge impact on how they view the organization, how motivated they are, and how long they are likely to remain an employee. Onboarding is much more than what many call an orientation, where new employees meet people, fill out lots of paperwork, and review the employee handbook.

It's good to have an onboarding philosophy rather than thinking of onboarding as a bunch of tasks that need to be accomplished. What is the objective when onboarding a new hire? What do you want them to know, feel, or do as a result of the onboarding process? Most employees want human connection for the first few days. They want to know that the organization wants them and is welcoming them in.

Much like business planning, it's best to begin with the objectives for your onboarding process. The structure and content should be driven by what you determine new hires need to understand about the organization and their role. Once you have this defined, you can create content that aligns with those objectives.

Consider the following questions:

- What do you want every new employee to know before they begin their new position? Consider company history, competitors, customers, industry trends, and so on.

- What information, resources, and contacts will the person need to be positioned to succeed in their job?

- If you were new to the company, what would you want to know that all existing employees already know to help them in effectively performing their jobs?

- How will the new person's performance be measured—what metrics will be used—and what is the current expected level of performance for each of those metrics?

- How can you help new employees understand what makes your company unique and better in the eyes of your customers? How would you describe what excellence means to you and what it looks like for each position?

- What information, company traditions, and stories should be related to new employees to help them better understand who you are, what your core values are, and how you treat and work with each other?

Onboarding Content and Schedule

Once the objectives are defined, create a schedule of subjects to be covered. Here's a checklist that can serve as a starting point.

Introduction to the Company

- Organization and its function
- Operations manual
- Company's position in the industry
- Company vision and mission
- Organizational goals

New Employee Paperwork

- W-4 and state tax forms
- I-9 forms
- Insurance enrollment forms

Compensation and Benefits

- Compensation agreement
- Salary increases/performance review process
- Incentive/bonus programs
- Pay procedures

Company Policies

- Anti-harassment

- Vacation and sick leave

- Attendance and punctuality standards

- Overtime

- Performance reviews

- Dress code

- Personal conduct standards

- Progressive disciplinary actions

- Confidentiality

- Email and Internet usage

- Safety and health rules

- Violence in the workplace

- Alcohol and drug usage

- Accidents and emergencies

Training Schedule

- Review training plan

Now consider the type of instruction to be employed for each topic and the amount of time needed to adequately cover the material, while allowing for hands-on experience or practice to verify that learning has taken place.

1. Assign responsibility to each area's hiring manager to draft an outline of the onboarding schedule for the first four weeks of a new employee's time in their area.

2. Remember to always include safety as a subject to be adequately covered during the onboarding period.

3. Be sure each topic included identifies the person best suited to deliver the information and answer questions.

4. Consider how learning will be measured—what methods will be used to test for understanding or to allow new employees to demonstrate their capabilities.

5. Ensure consistency in the way all new hires are being onboarded, regardless of which department they are in.

6. Along with the HR representative, be sure the leadership team has reviewed and either revised or approved each onboarding schedule.

When creating the onboarding schedule for a given department, consider the following when determining how much time to allocate for each subject.

- An existing training program, class, or online instruction will likely include a predetermined amount of time for training and testing. Use this time, but also remember to include travel time, if needed.

- Allow time for any preparation or reading when there is material the employee needs to view on their own before discussing with someone or moving to another topic.

- When training involves learning a process and applying it on the job, be sure to allow time for both instruction and practical application. This might include working with another team member on actual job sites and having that team member provide the new hire with explanations and feedback. If multiple real-world sessions are needed, be sure to plan enough time for them.

- Consider the availability of anyone serving as an instructor or resource. Be sure to consult with them about their availability in advance and confirm in person before committing to the schedule.

- Remember to include travel time to and from jobs when on-site training or experience is included as part of the onboarding.

In the midst of trying to get a lot of information to new employees, it's easy to overlook the fact that they will have questions and can offer valuable feedback as they go through the onboarding process. Be sure to allow plenty of time for this in the schedule.

Safety

The onboarding schedule for all new hires should include safety material, and every new employee should be given a safety orientation before beginning work. Refer to the **New Employee Safety Orientation Checklist** in the online Appendix as a guide that provides a sample list of the topics to be covered.

Identify the Players

Once you identify the objectives and content for onboarding, the next step is to identify those who will develop and present the material. Use the onboarding checklist you created to assign responsibilities for each element. Remember that someone needs to take care of the overall planning and scheduling for the onboarding period, making sure all participants are aware of and prepared for their segment.

For many of the topics related to the overall company and administrative elements, the participants may be the same for all new hires. Subject matter that is more specific to the department or job the new person is taking on will likely involve different employees.

It is critical that the business owner be involved in the onboarding process. They should be welcoming all new employees to the organization on their first day and personally conducting conversations on mission, vision, core values, and company culture. New hires need to hear this information from the source, which is the leader of the organization.

Some companies use "buddies" or mentors as part of the onboarding process. These peers are actively involved in making sure the new person gets the tools, information, and resources they need to be successful.

Schedule

Creating the overall schedule is a critical part of onboarding planning. New employees expect to know what they will be doing for the first 2 or 3 weeks, up to the first 90 days. There is nothing more impressive to a new employee than being presented with a detailed schedule of how they will spend the first three to five days of their employment and what the next month or two looks like in more general terms.

Ideally, new hires will be provided with an itinerary for the first few days, at least, in advance of their start date. Plan to make information such as your mission statement, vision statement, core values, and even your employee handbook or policy available to them in advance. This allows them to review the information on their own time and be better prepared for sessions covering those topics.

Teaching and Learning

The following general categories should be covered in the onboarding process:

- Company overview

- General information

- Receive the new employee

- Welcome the new employee

- Show the new employee around

- Introduce the new employee

While the purpose of many of the individual sessions is to share information with or explain things to the new person, it is also important to take advantage of opportunities to learn about them. This will allow you to …

- become more familiar with the person's experience, training, and education

- discover the employee's career goals and objectives

- gather any information they may have regarding any of the company's vendors or primary competitors

Onboarding Follow-Up and Assessment

The best source for feedback on the effectiveness of your onboarding process is employees who have recently gone through it. Give them enough time to realistically assess how well-prepared they were for their job.

1. Target three to six months after completion of onboarding to perform the follow-up.

2. Inform new employees as they are going through the onboarding process that you will be asking for their feedback and ideas for improvement after a few months on the job.

3. Be sure to give new hires immediate and ongoing feedback on their performance. Don't wait three to six months to tell them how they're doing and where improvements are needed. The formal follow-up session then provides the opportunity to give them even more feedback.

At the same time, don't ignore the value of getting feedback in real time from those who are going through the onboarding process. If you want to increase retention, it's always good to measure while the process is happening.

Based on an adequate level of feedback, hiring managers are responsible for recommending appropriate changes to the onboarding schedule or content.

Tracking Performance

It is important to be able to track performance to measure the impact of changes you have made that are pertinent to the subject of your onboarding process. When using these or other key performance indicators to track performance improvement, be sure to measure your current performance, perhaps going back in time a year or two, to set a baseline. Then track the same metrics after you implement your changes to verify that you are achieving the intended results.

In your annual business planning process, include setting targets or goals for the coming year for the chosen metrics. Here are some examples:

Turnover (annual)—percentage of total employees who leave the organization during a given year divided by the average actual number of employees during the same period.

Owner Onboarding—number of hours invested by the business owner or CEO in new employee onboarding during the previous year.

Engagement or Satisfaction Rating—percent of employees who rate themselves as engaged or satisfied overall with a given aspect of the workplace.

CHAPTER 7

Owner Impact

Small businesses are a reflection of their owner(s). Employees, especially high-performing employees, will choose to work with people who exhibit the qualities and characteristics that align with their own values. This is why the information below, and the behavior of the owner in general, can have a significant impact on recruiting and retention.

If the owner's leadership style, ego, and behavior reflect qualities and attitudes that are deemed by candidates as being negative or not conducive to their own personal and professional growth, they are less likely to seek employment with that company or to stay on board if they have already been hired.

The Emotionally Intelligent Leader

Most of the business owners we've worked with at Violand Management are smart, sincere, and hard-working individuals. They've muscled their company's growth through a combination of sweat, adrenalin, working insane hours, and luck. Most have not yet developed what business guru Jim Collins would call Level 5 Leadership skills: a powerful combination of personal humility and indomitable will. As a result, they struggle with attracting and keeping the level of talent needed to continue growing their expanding business.

It's common to see these owners' hiring decisions either being driven by or at least affected by entrepreneurial behavior such as micromanaging, conflict avoidance, lack of follow-through, an oversized ego, or a noxious combination of all.

In extreme cases, we've seen where "the word on the street" spread that these companies are not desirable places to work, making it extremely difficult to attract competent talent. Worse still, if we're able to help them hire someone, it frequently isn't long before they realize the company isn't a place they want to work and they leave. While this situation doesn't always lead to a company's failure, it almost always causes the company's growth to stall, as they aren't able to attract the needed talent.

Contrast the above situation with that of a company led by an owner who is intentionally developing their leadership skills. While they may not have achieved Level 5 status yet, they are aware of the skills needed to lead their growing company. They also recognize the impact their negative behaviors have on their company and its ability to attract top talent and they work to manage those behaviors.

These become companies whose positive reputations grow in the areas they serve, and their employees and community members recommend them. A pleasant bonus is that this not only attracts good employees but also attracts customers. These are companies where workers and customers feel their opinions are heard, where they are empowered to make decisions, and where they feel appreciated.

Our experience has shown that companies led by emotionally intelligent owners enjoy stronger growth, profitability, and employee retention over a longer period. Their strong financial performance is no doubt helped by their ability to hold onto experienced workers, thus reducing the need to recruit and train a revolving door of new people.

Much has been written about the growing impact of emotional intelligence in the workplace. The following is extracted from the article "Emotional Intelligence: One of the Keys to a Healthy Company Culture" written by my colleague, Tom Cline.

> As teamwork and collaboration are becoming more important to how organizations produce work, make decisions, and improve processes, the ability of all employees to understand EQ concepts and appropriately adapt their behaviors can be critical to a healthy culture and the attraction and retention of top talent.
>
> Let's begin by reviewing a brief background on the four characteristics that most experts agree are at the core of emotional intelligence.
>
> 1. **Self-awareness**—Thoroughly understanding yourself and your effect on others. Those who are self-aware know their abilities, play to their strengths, and welcome feedback. They typically

have a self-deprecating sense of humor; they admit to failure and do it with a smile.

2. **Self-regulation**—Controlling destructive impulses and thinking before acting. This involves fairness and trust when interacting with others and focusing on addressing the reasons for failure instead of placing blame.

Experts describe these first two traits as our "personal competence." It represents our ability to stay aware of our emotions and manage our behavior and tendencies.

The remaining traits are those that make up our "social competence"—our ability to understand other people's moods, behaviors, and motives in order to improve the quality of our relationships. They are:

3. **Social awareness**—The ability to accurately pick up on emotions in other people and understand what's really going on.

4. **Relationship management**—The ability to use your awareness of your own emotions and those of others to successfully manage interactions.

For more on the topic of emotional intelligence and some of the entrepreneurial behaviors mentioned here, refer to the **Overcoming Stage 2 Stall** booklet and **Emotional Intelligence: One of the Keys to a Healthy Company Culture** article in the online Appendix.

Mission and Vision

The business owner or president sets the tone, demeanor, and character for the entire business. In a publicly held company, this is done by the CEO. This positioning, while not necessarily in the strict marketing sense, begins with the organization's mission and vision, as these are statements and ideas that come primarily from the owner or CEO and address two different aspects of the broad view of the company.

1. **Mission**—the mission statement, or what is sometimes referred to as the Core Purpose, is at the heart of any organization. It answers the question "Why?" Why do you do what you do? Why would

your customers miss you if you were not here? The concept of mission is much broader than just describing what your company does or what it makes.

Part of what the owner or CEO should describe is what it looks like when the company and its employees are living the mission or demonstrating its core purpose.

2. **Vision**—often called the vision statement, it is a description of what you aspire to become, achieve, or create. It is a long-term view that should be out of reach at the present but not out of sight. Your vision should also address the question "What does winning look like for your company?" It is about picking a destination that will stimulate enthusiasm about change and progress.

    Accompanying the destination—where you see your business in 10 years or so—is what is called "vivid descriptions." These are statements evoking passion and emotion that describe what it will be like when the vision is reached.

Owners and CEOs are the flag bearers and cheerleaders for the mission and vision. They should be the visionaries of the business. They should constantly reinforce these ideas and be sure that shorter-term strategies and decisions are aligned with the firm's purpose and ultimate destination.

Core Values

Your organization is a living, breathing organism with a distinct personality that is expressed through its core values. Those values are the soul of the organization. They describe the rules, culture, and personality of the company. Core values are the ideals the company stands for even when it feels risky or uncomfortable to do so. By definition, you and your people will follow these values even if they become a competitive disadvantage.

As the chief advocate of the company's core values, the owner and their behavior, demeanor, priorities, and treatment of others are viewed by employees as the ultimate role model. When employees see the core values being lived and respected every day by the owner and leaders in the organization, trust is built. They perceive high levels of ethics and integrity in those who "practice what they preach."

If there is an inconsistency between the espoused values or culture and how the owner runs the business, determines priorities, and treats others, employees will lose trust. The result is them behaving in ways they see as being in their best interest. They will choose to either leave the organization or adapt to the actual values and then be driven by self-preservation.

An explanation of the organization's core values and how they influence the culture should be an integral part of the recruiting and hiring process. Candidates who cannot commit to behaving and working in accordance with those values should not be considered a good fit for hiring.

Constant attention is required for both keeping mission, vision, and core values up to date and communicating them to all employees. Reviewing, discussing, and updating these statements should happen on at least an annual basis. Actual examples of employees living the mission and demonstrating the core values should be solicited and reviewed. Employees should be publicly praised when they are seen exemplifying what the organization is all about. Any changes or additions to the mission, vision, and core values should be reviewed with all team members, explaining the reasons behind the change.

Leadership

A critical part of any business owner's role is that of leadership, and leadership is shown in a number of ways. As described above, people lead in the sense that they provide the overall direction for the business; the vision for where it is going. They provide leadership in how they treat, respect, communicate with, and are committed to developing people. When owners belittle their employees and generally treat them as a cost to be managed rather than an asset, good people don't join the team. And if they do, they don't stay.

People are leaders in that they are viewed by employees as someone to be emulated, someone who shows respect and is respected. They make a promise to always lean into leading, knowing that there is no neutral stance that can be taken when serving as a leader. They are those to whom employees turn in times of chaos and strife. Effective leaders create a culture that reflects their own beliefs and values.

Leadership includes continuing to develop yourself. Sometimes owners resist this out of fear of change and fear of the unknown. If we continue to develop ourselves as leaders, what changes might this bring to our company and what new and uncomfortable demands might this place on us as owners?

The following is an excerpt from my *Overcoming Stage 2 Stall* booklet.

When things are going well in our company, it's easy to convince ourselves that we have all the answers and don't need to continue growing as leaders. Rather than exploring new ideas, investigating promising markets for our services, or driving more-efficient ways to deliver our services, we play the mental equivalent of computer solitaire. We keep playing the same game over and over and settle for an occasional win. When this happens, it doesn't take long for competitors, market changes, or technological advances to catch up and send our company into a stall.

We fear change. While this may not be a major factor when a company is young, it's not uncommon for it to occur as the business owner ages. The exhilaration felt from trying new things and rapid growth can sometimes wane as we get older. As a result, we may not be as willing to gamble the groceries on a new idea. In the later stages of our business, we usually have more to protect or more to lose if our gamble doesn't pan out.

The complete **Overcoming Stage 2 Stall** booklet can be found in the online Appendix.

Trust

The culture of an organization results from a combination of values and behaviors. Building a culture based on trust takes a lot of work. It starts by creating an environment where people feel safe and comfortable being themselves. People will trust their leaders when the leaders do the things that make them feel psychologically safe. Giving managers and employees discretion in how they do the job they have been trained to do is an example.

Conversely, when leaders place excessive stress on people to "make the numbers" and may offer lopsided incentive structures to reinforce it, they risk the decline of long-term performance, trust, psychological safety, and the will of the people. Ethical lapses on the part of employees may begin to appear and may be overlooked by leadership as part of the win-at-all-costs mentality. When these elements are present, several negative things occur:

- **Performance declines**—employees who are stressed at work perform more poorly.

- **Trust is undermined**—people behave in support of their own best interests, even at the expense of other employees and the overall interests of the business.

- **Bureaucracy increases**—in weak cultures people find safety in the rules. This damages the trust inside and outside an organization.

Micromanaging

Micromanaging is, by definition, controlling every part of an activity or enterprise, no matter how small. In business, it is looking over the shoulder of every manager and employee to ensure that every decision made, every task completed, and every piece of output meets the expectation of the micromanager. To the people being managed this is frustrating, demoralizing, and demotivating. It is a clear sign that your boss or owner doesn't trust you. It also creates an unhealthy dependency that has the owner tied to every aspect of the company, which ultimately stifles growth.

Many entrepreneurs have controlling personalities that put them at a high risk of micromanaging. After all, many of them launched their company so they could control their own environment and destiny. The same can be said for some managers. The following example illustrates this point.

Micromanagement and Unclear Expectations

A case that highlights the pitfalls of micromanaging is "Bob," a business owner who had a five-year-old business that stalled. He and his partner had grown revenue to $1.5 million by year three. Then it plateaued. In addition to his partner's ineptitude, Bob was famous for "over promising and under delivering"—especially to his employees. Turnover was very high. People came on board, learned how things were under Bob's leadership, and many left. A lack of management controls meant things were in disarray. Managers and employees didn't know what was expected of them, and they didn't know how the business was doing. The Administration and Operations managers were good people, but Bob didn't let them run their departments. He made the decisions, so employees regularly went to him instead of their manager for approvals and decisions.

Working with Violand Management, Bob bought out his partner, put appropriate management controls and reporting in place, and was persuaded to let his managers run their departments. And they shined! Responsibilities and authority are now clearly defined. The business is once again growing and it is profitable. When the owner understood the effect his micromanaging was having, he was able to step back and let his people do their jobs.

While many may not even realize they are micromanaging, here are some of the clear signs:

- You are never quite satisfied with deliverables (what your people produce or decide).

- You often feel frustrated because you would have gone about the task differently.

- You are laser-focused on the details and take great pride in making corrections to other people's work.

- You constantly want to know where all your team members are and what they are working on.

- You don't delegate tasks, thinking no one can do things as well as you.

- You ask for frequent updates on where things stand.

- You want to "protect" others from being overworked, so you do everything yourself.

- You become the bottleneck that slows progress and timeliness.

- You prefer to be cc'd on all emails and correspondence.

Chronic micromanagers say: "Too much is at stake to allow this to go wrong." What they really mean is: "I don't trust them to do their jobs according to my standards." Often underlying the need to micromanage is a fear of failure (Nothing's going to go wrong on my watch!). By magnifying the risk of failure, your employees engage in "learned helplessness" where they begin to believe that the only way they can perform is if you micromanage them. It's a vicious cycle.

To overcome micromanaging behavior, try the following:

- Give the what, not the how. There is nothing wrong with having expectations about a deliverable, but there's a difference between sharing those expectations and dictating how to get the result. Articulate what you envision the final outcome to look like and then let the person do it their way.

- Expect to win most of the time. Set up your direct reports for success and be clear on what success looks like. Provide needed resources, information, and support. A loss every now and then helps build a strong track record in the long run.

- Train your people to perform tasks the way your company needs them and to follow the processes you have in place.

- Let go of the minutia. Look at your to-do list and decide what can be passed off to another team member. Spend most of your time on the big-ticket items where you truly add value.

- Give credit where credit is due.

- Focus on seeing the big picture and motivating your people.

Accountability

As the owner or CEO, you cannot and should not perform or be involved in every task that takes place in the business. Not being involved in every decision or verifying the outcome of every task—in other words, not micromanaging—is about delegating authority and responsibility to others. As the business grows, you delegate to others the responsibility for more and more tasks and decisions and they become the owners of those tasks. But this does not mean that people should not be held accountable.

Accountability refers to being answerable for our actions. An employee may be responsible for making sure there are adequate office supplies. They are aware of the task and will continue to order supplies as needed to avoid running out. The employee is held accountable—owing an explanation for their actions—if supplies ever run out.

Effective leadership involves delegating responsibility to others; making sure they understand what is expected; providing the training, resources, and time for them to be successful; and holding them accountable for the results. Lack of accountability results in a lack of urgency, focus, and follow-through.

Ego

An inflated ego corrupts our behavior. When we believe we're the sole architects of our success, we tend to be rude, more selfish, and more likely to interrupt others. An inflated ego prevents us from learning from our mistakes and creates a defensive wall that makes it difficult to appreciate the lessons we glean from failure. Those with oversized egos often feel their position excuses them from having to ask permission, show gratitude, or apologize.

A swollen ego has a debilitating effect on an owner's hearing. They have no interest in considering input from others, because they believe they already have all the answers. Warren Bennis, a pioneer in the field of leadership, writes "Authentic leaders ... don't have what people in the Middle East called 'tired ears'."

When challenged by an employee with a different perspective or decision, the ego-driven owner or executive uses their title or position as the reason for not taking that person's suggestion. Soon, people stop coming up with ideas because they know they will be ignored. This is not a recipe for developing an empowered workplace.

The combination of false pride and self-doubt created by an overactive ego gives people a distorted image of their own importance. They see themselves as the center of the universe and begin to put their own agenda, safety, status, and gratification ahead of the company and the people affected by their thoughts and actions.

Clear signs of ego affliction include:

- Spending more time promoting yourself than discussing other people's ideas

- Being fearful of mistakes

- Making excuses when your ideas don't pan out as expected

- Avoiding certain members of your team—particularly people you feel are especially smart and talented

- Refusing to accept evidence that you are wrong and placing blame on other people or things

Learning to put aside your ego can be enhanced by practicing the following:

- **Give praise**—practice giving credit to others.

- **Seek mentorship**—to act as mentors, find three people you can trust to tell you the truth even when it hurts. Make a commitment to listen to their opinions.

- **Learn**—focus on skills you'd like to learn from each of your employees and make a commitment to learn them.

- **Recognize behavior**—overcoming an overactive ego is about humility and self-regulation. Humility means recognizing that work is not all about you. It's about the people you serve and what they need.

- **Be vulnerable**—show your humanity and willingness to learn and grow from your mistakes.

- **Create a vision**—a way to achieve healthy organizational collaboration and minimize individual ego is to rally people around a shared vision. (Refer to Chapter 3 on Company Culture.)

Impacts on hiring and retention are as follows:

1. If you insist on being the smartest person in the room, or you feel threatened by having people smarter than you on the team, you will undermine hiring talented people whether consciously or subconsciously. Instead, you will come up with a litany of reasons why they aren't a good fit.

2. Ego can stop you from asking for input from others and, instead, cause you to make knee-jerk decisions and take unnecessary risks. High-performing employees see this behavior and question the long-term viability of the business. Yours is not an organization they will commit to for very long.

3. In his book, *How the Mighty Fall,* Jim Collins describes "hubris born of success." He explains that the egos and arrogance of company leaders can cause them to believe they're entitled to success and that the rules of business no longer apply to them. They mistakenly believe they are insulated from the risk of failure.

   My work with small businesses has shown me that when the owner's ego is out of control, it's not a matter of IF the company will stall or decline, it's a matter of WHEN. If not based solely on the leader's behavior and ego, then at the first sign of its impact on the business, "A" players will flee what they see as the sinking ship.

Personal Interest

People want to feel that they are valued for more than just the work they perform. A critical element in a positive company culture is that employees feel like their employer cares about them as human beings. While regular conversations with your people regarding the status of their work, level of quality, resources, and potential roadblocks are expected and perfectly reasonable, taking a personal interest in each of them takes little time from an owner's or manager's day but is extremely powerful and well worth the time.

Taking a personal interest in your team members is as simple as taking time to do the following:

- Get to know every employee. The owner should welcome every new employee on their first day and be armed with some personal information about them to include during the conversation.

- Take the time to simply say "Hello" to every person you encounter during the workday. Ask some of them how they are doing—and do so with the intent of truly understanding how they are feeling that day.

- Ask if you can help. When talking to employees about work, ask if there is anything you can do to help them remove barriers or increase the likelihood of their success.

- Learn about people's families and interests. Find out what they do when they are not at work. Ask about events, family trips, and children's activities.

- Wish people "Happy Birthday" in person.

Showing interest in people has a significant impact on hiring and retention. When you don't take an interest in others because you are dealing with an oversized ego (they might be having more fun than you or be more successful) you may not be aware of how little interest you show in others. The owner wanting to know or learn about an employee can be highly motivating. Regularly taking a personal interest or asking if there is something you can do to help the employee succeed, or both, will cause the employee's spirits to soar.

Tracking Progress

It is important to be able to track performance to measure the impact of changes you have made that are pertinent to the subject of owner impact. When using these or other key performance indicators to track performance improvement, be sure to measure your current performance, perhaps going back in time a year or two, to set a baseline. Then track the same metrics after you implement your changes to verify that you are achieving the intended results.

In your annual business planning process, include setting targets or goals for the coming year for the chosen metrics. Here are some examples:

Turnover (annual)—number of employees leaving the organization during a 12-month period divided by the average actual number of employees during the same period.

Suggestion Implementation—number of employee improvement suggestions implemented divided by the total number of suggestions received.

Revenue Per Employee—total company revenue divided by number of employees (annual).

Profitability—gross profit or net profit as a percentage of revenue.

Capital Reinvestment—percentage of net profit reinvested into the business through capital assets, training, and professional development.

Training/Development Hours—sum of total training hours for all employees divided by the total number of employees.

CHAPTER 8

Performance Management

Quite a bit of confusion exists around the term *performance management*—much of it centered around the idea of a performance review, which is only one element in the overall process.

The following quote from Patrick Lencioni's book, *The Advantage: Why Organizational Health Trumps Everything Else in Business*, does a great job of simplifying and explaining this critical organizational activity: "Essentially performance management is the series of activities that ensures that managers provide employees with clarity about what is expected of them, as well as regular feedback about whether they are adequately meeting those expectations."

Performance Management

Performance management begins with expectations. You cannot evaluate performance without the benchmark of what is expected. Management's job is to establish and continually reinforce expectations, to clearly communicate those expectations, and to provide their people with the tools, resources, and training to set them up for success. And then they must hold them accountable.

The first piece to put in place is a written job description. Each position should have one. It describes the overall purpose of the position, areas of responsibility and authority, and how performance will be measured, among other elements. On the next page is a portion of a formal job description for the position of bookkeeper.

For any position in an organization, performance expectations consist of two elements: the metrics or criteria that will be used to measure performance and the accompanying goals or targets—the specific values to be achieved for a defined time period. Metrics used are less

Bookkeeper Position Description

Job Title:	Bookkeeper	Status:	Non-Exempt
Department/Group:	Administration	Travel Required:	No
Position Reports to:	Administration Manager	Position Type:	Full-Time
Salaried/Hourly:	Hourly		
Reporting Positions:			

Approved By:		Date:	
Updated By:		Date:	

Position Summary/Purpose

Assist in the profitable growth of the company and provide support to management through the accurate and timely performance of bookkeeping functions.

Help retain customers by providing emotional support through phone conversations, follow-up contacts, and the accurate and timely transcription of customer information.

Primary Duties and Responsibilities

- Accurate and timely invoicing of customers.
- Complete job costing on completed work.
- Make deposits to company bank accounts.
- Conduct follow-up phone calls to customers and collection calls on overdue invoices.
- Prepare and file tax forms.
- Maintain office inventory.

Figure 8.1 Position description

likely to change, whereas the goals may adjust from year to year based on the organization's business plan, the experience level of the business development rep, and other factors like services offered and target markets.

An example of performance expectations for a business development rep might be that they are evaluated on the revenue generated by the referral sources they call on and the number of formal meetings they hold with customers and prospects. Both of these can be measured monthly and annually. Goals or targets for these metrics might be annual revenue of $1 million and 20 meetings each month.

Blind Eye Management

We've seen countless examples over the years of clients who, when asked if they hold their people accountable, respond with "Absolutely!" or "Of course we do." Upon closer examination, the truth is that employees are described as being "good with customers" or having "unique technical abilities" that serve the company well. These and other subjective descriptions are indicators of the true situation—that leadership looks only at the positive aspects of an employee's abilities and performance and doesn't address the areas needing improvement. It also likely means that metrics aren't in place to measure performance or there aren't clear expectations for what the level of performance should be.

This scenario can be fueled by an owner who accepts mediocre answers because they prefer to avoid hearing bad news about performance, which is uncomfortable and leads to further uncomfortable conversations.

Not only does this mean that specific managers or employees aren't being held accountable, but it also means that others in the organization are likely being impacted by the poor performance. For instance, when the person responsible for invoicing customers after services are provided or a job is closed isn't doing their job, cash flow is impacted, revenue figures are inaccurate, and salespeople may be missing out on commissions.

Retaining high-performing employees is based on accountability. When accountability is lacking, especially when it is being driven by the owner, there is usually a chain reaction. It starts when the "A" players are performing well, while some of the other employees are not. With no accountability, there are no repercussions for the low performers. When your best people see this, they will eventually either reduce their level of output or leave the company.

Corollary: When these organizations begin to address the situation, put a performance management system in place, and start to hold their people accountable, it makes some employees uncomfortable. In many cases, these are tenured employees whose typical response to questions like "How are we doing?" or "Are we in good shape?" elicits responses along the lines of "We're good" or "I've got it under control." Probing for details or facts to back up their assessment leads to "I've been doing this for years and we've been fine" or words to that effect. When that person is then faced with metrics, data, and objective measures of performance, their reaction may be to leave the company. These folks can be longtime friends of the owner or even relatives who have been awakened from their comfort zone.

High Tide Conceals the Rocks

We were brought in to work with a company that had been doing over $20 million in revenue annually. In the period leading up to our engagement, the company went from respectable profitability to posting a net loss of just under $1 million in less than 12 months. What happened? A combination of factors caused the near demise of the business. The root cause was the lack of a performance management system, resulting in a lack of accountability. Previously, an ongoing series of large, unexpected, and highly profitable contracts had kept the cash flowing and the company in the black. When those jobs were no longer coming in, the "rocks" or weaknesses nearly took down the ship. Cash flow dried up, and the situation was critical.

From the owners and throughout the management team, there was little accountability. No targets or budgets were established. No revenue expectations were set. No profitability goals were in place. Project managers ran projects as they chose, and there were no ramifications when jobs weren't profitable. One particular business development rep brought in a number of the larger jobs, while two others generated little in revenue. When asked what metrics were used to track and measure the company's performance, the president of the company could only come up with "cash in the bank!"

This company needed to change before its ship sank. Fortunately, there was a change agent among the ranks—a bright, young accountant with a track record for results and the drive and desire to match. With a little guidance and a lot of support, he took the helm (under duress) and immediately shifted the emphasis from top-line volume to bottom-line results.

Generating cash flow, creating an effective management team, and putting performance management systems in place were the top priorities. Overhead costs were slashed, owners' salaries dialed back, executive positions eliminated, and significant changes in other management roles were implemented. A short-term business plan was created with metrics, specific targets, and timely, continuous follow-up. Performance expectations were established for every department: profitability goals were set by job type; revenue expectations were created for each sales rep; and cash flow, a receivables level, and debt reduction targets were put in place. A leadership team was created and met frequently to track performance, provide direction, and prioritize the subsequent steps needed to right the ship.

Fortunately, once again, several significant contracts were secured, and the company also signed a large institutional job over the next 18 months. This time, performance expectations were clear. Documented processes were followed in operations, finance, administration, and marketing. Progress and results were tracked through the timely review of metrics. Corrections and adjustments were made as needed.

The phrase "a rising tide lifts all boats" is appropriate here. Without a performance management system in place, the company had been plodding along, thanks to a consistent flow of revenue. When that dried up, the situation quickly became critical. Performance management helped the owners to right-size the organization, put the right people in positions of responsibility, and significantly improve the overall performance of the business.

Focus on Performance

Focusing on performance management in your business doesn't need to be complicated. Here are the most important things to consider when doing so:

- Create written job descriptions for each position, outlining areas of responsibility and authority.

- Establish appropriate metrics for each position.

- Define the expectations for performance—the goals or targets.

- Clearly communicate position-specific performance expectations to all employees.

- Create a feedback culture where it's customary for employees to receive either motivational or developmental feedback on

how they are doing on a regular basis; don't wait for an annual
performance review to point out areas where changes are needed.

- Gather employee input as part of the performance assessment
  process.

- Agree with each employee on areas where additional training or
  development is needed and establish a plan for making it happen.

It's important to think broadly about the elements of your business that
should be covered by the metrics used in measuring performance. Financial
and operational metrics are most often in place because they are more easily measured, and the data is already being captured. Be sure to also track
your performance in other areas like customer satisfaction, the state of your
internal processes and systems, and staff alignment and development.

Evaluation Checklist

To assess the current state of your performance management system, use
the following as a checklist for what you should have in place:

- Accurate and up-to-date job descriptions

- A selection and hiring process to ensure you are hiring the
  best candidates possible

- Performance standards and expectations that match what is
  needed in the business

- Measurements to track performance against established
  standards or expectations

- A focus on appropriate employee onboarding, training, and
  ongoing development

- Training for employees that includes both technical
  (functional) and soft skills, including management

- Continual coaching and feedback—MBWA (Management by
  Walking Around)

- Quarterly performance development discussions with employees covering both past behaviors and future expectations

- Effective compensation and recognition systems that reward people for their contributions

- Promotion, leadership, and career development opportunities for your people

- Exit interviews to assess the reasons why valued employees are leaving

Formal Performance Evaluation

When conducted properly, employee performance reviews provide employees with vital feedback on their performance and serve as part of a structured approach to continual improvement. The objective is to provide support to employees by providing them with a planned approach to clarify what is expected of them, provide feedback on their performance, and create a platform for continued performance improvement.

Formal employee evaluations are an important part of every manager's role and are vital to effectively developing, managing, and motivating everyone in your organization. All employees, regardless of position, should have a performance review meeting with their direct supervisor twice per year or, at a minimum, once per year.

Refer to the online Appendix for an **Employee Evaluation Form**.

Conducting employee performance reviews can be a sensitive and emotionally draining experience for both the employee and the manager. In our experience, a manager's lack of training, and therefore resistance to conducting formal review meetings, is often the reason for reviews not taking place. When managers are properly trained, fear and hesitation are usually replaced with a positive attitude. Once employees see that the focus of the process is to help them to succeed, not berate them for every mistake they make, the positive vibe will continue. By following a consistent process, stress will be reduced for both parties involved and help make the review a positive, constructive experience.

Figure 8.2 *Employee evaluation*

Instant Performance Evaluations

Understand that providing feedback and assessments to employees regarding their performance is something that should happen on an ongoing basis and not be reserved for a twice-per-year, formal performance review. Both praising an employee for work well done and pointing out areas where their performance needs to improve are important parts of every manager's daily job. This feedback should occur whenever an observed activity warrants it. Each of these opportunities, whether positive or negative, should be documented with the date and a brief note describing the situation that was discussed with the employee. These instances should be referred to in support of the "progress made" or "improvement needed" sections of their performance review. The formal review, therefore, should not contain any information regarding an employee's performance that they haven't already heard.

The System Is the Solution

When clients have heeded our counsel and put effective performance management systems in place, the impact is transformative. Going from an environment with no defined expectations, no data, and little account-ability to one where performance is fact-based makes a world of differ-ence. Here's where they end up: expectations are set, meaning the metrics are defined and goals are established—not only for financial performance but for all critical areas of the business. These include financial, customer satisfaction, processes and systems, and staff alignment and development. The necessary tools and resources are provided to employees, people are held accountable, praise is given when performance is good, and feedback is delivered for areas where improvement is needed. There are ramifica-tions for people's performance. Rewards are given on the positive side, and discipline is applied when efforts to improve results are ineffective.

Compensation models are based on performance, not longevity as is the case in businesses without performance management systems. Employees who perform well are rewarded. Ultimately, people who can't meet the performance expectations leave the company.

There are also noticeable differences in the leadership and manage-ment of performance-driven businesses. While leaders may not have all the answers, they know what the right questions are, and those questions are based on metrics or key performance indicators. "How are we doing?" is replaced with "What are our gross profit results compared to targets for the first quarter?" or "Are we meeting our goals in customer satisfaction ratings?"

These transitions don't happen overnight, but neither do they take years. Focused efforts to identify the right metrics, collect actual perfor-mance data, and set appropriate targets, along with training managers in performance evaluation and daily communication can lead to having an effective performance management system in place within a 12-month period.

Coaching

Coaching employees and managers is an important element in the per-formance management system. Those who are responsible for other employees should be trained in and regularly practice the concept of coaching their people. This should be a normal part of the day-to-day interaction between an employee and their manager or a manager and their superior.

The goal of coaching is to work with the employee to solve performance problems and to improve the output of the employee, the team, and the department. Regular coaching brings performance issues to the employee's attention while they are still minor. Providing feedback helps the employee to correct the issues before they significantly reduce their performance.

It's important to recognize the considerable difference between coaching and managing:

- Coaching is developmental, having more to do with asking, listening, and suggesting. Managing is problem solving, dealing with measuring, evaluating, and directing.

- Coaching is nondirective and focuses on drawing out solutions. Managing is directive and focuses on putting in the solutions.

- Coaching results in the person being coached increasing their self-awareness and willingness to be accountable for the outcomes. Managing maintains most of the responsibilities because it's their ideas.

- Coaching is about supporting the person in identifying answers that lead to change. Managing is about establishing performance expectations and measuring progress toward them.

Tracking Performance

It is important to be able to track performance to measure the impact of changes you have made that are pertinent to the subject of performance management. When using these or other key performance indicators to track performance improvement, be sure to measure your current performance, perhaps going back in time a year or two, to set a baseline. Then track the same metrics after you implement your changes to verify that you are achieving the intended results.

In your annual business planning process, include setting targets or goals for the coming year for chosen metrics. Here are some examples:

Performance Rating Participation Rate—number of employees who have been given a specific score or rating on their performance evaluation divided by the total number of employees.

Position Performance Measurement—percentage of total positions (titles) within the organization for which metrics are defined for measuring performance AND goals or expectations for current year performance have been established and communicated to the employee(s).

CHAPTER 9

Policies, Practices, and Procedures

This chapter is about documenting the way you do things in your business. We'll begin by explaining what we mean by the terms.

Policies—these are the written rules for behavior, attire, and all the laws and regulations that apply to the workplace. They cover topics from paid time off to discipline, safety, a drug-free workplace, and employee benefits. Every employee should have an up-to-date copy of your employee policies.

Practices—this is what you actually do. While they may not be in writing, when you respond to a certain situation the same way over and over, in a legal sense, it defines a policy or an expectation. For example, there may not be anything in writing that says you have an operations meeting every Thursday at 8:00 a.m., but you've been doing it for years, so those employees who are part of the meeting are expected to be there. For topics covered by written policies or procedures, it is important that what you actually do is consistent with what's in writing. When actual practice is inconsistent with what's in writing, the "practice" is what counts from a legal perspective.

Procedures—these are the written instructions for how your services are provided or how specific tasks are completed. The instructions may take multiple forms, including flowcharts, workflow diagrams, videos, written step-by-step instructions, process maps, or photos. Documents, forms, templates, and reports may be included or referenced in some procedures.

Why Go to the Trouble to Document All of This?

"So, what if we don't have all our processes and procedures written down? We do these things all the time. We know how they're done."

There are many benefits to having documented (and regularly updated) policies, practices, and procedures, but these are the most significant:

Fairness—having written employee policies on everything from work attire to vacations to employee discipline means that everyone understands the same expectations and everyone is treated under the same set of rules. They provide guardrails for employees, so they know where the boundaries are. And the boundaries don't change unless we tell them they've changed.

Consistency—whether it is employee policies or the procedures for how services are provided, when it is written down, everyone is expected to do things the same way. This results in consistency. It stops things being done one way today and a different way tomorrow. Being consistent creates a culture where people are not treated differently and this is important from a liability standpoint.

Training—how the work should be done is written down. Whether in the form of a flowchart, procedure, or process map, it should be this information that is used to train people on that particular task. Whether it's answering the phone or posting invoices in an accounting system, the documented process is what you use every time someone needs to be trained on how to perform that job.

Quality and Efficiency—when you decide what the best way is to perform a certain job, that's what you document and capture as the official process or procedure. If you come up with a better or more effective way to complete a task, you change or update the procedure and let everyone know there is a new version. That way everyone is working with the most up-to-date process that will produce the highest quality, most-efficient result.

Relationship to Hiring and Retaining People

What do relationships have to do with hiring and retention? The advantages listed above are all elements that high-performing people are looking for in their work environment.

Consider the following:

- If employee policies aren't documented and people are treated differently, it's difficult to develop a culture of trust.

- If I get trained by Joe and you get trained by Sue and we learn how to do the same thing differently, which is better? Who decides? Some customers may be satisfied while others may not.

- As our knowledge grows or as technology changes and there are better ways to do things, we need to be sure that everyone is trained on what the changes are. The company and our customers will realize the benefits from those changes every time we perform the job.

- When it comes to accountability, it's difficult to hold people accountable for behaving as expected or performing tasks in the correct way if the rules aren't written down. "A" players want to be held accountable.

Start With Employee Policies

When it comes to having documentation for your business, the highest priority is the policies you apply in recruiting, hiring, and employing your people. Lack of written policies can result in everything from unfair and inconsistent treatment of employees to legal challenges and lawsuits.

The centerpiece of employee policies and procedures is your employee handbook or employee policy document. This document should be reviewed periodically by a human resources professional or labor attorney who is familiar with state and local laws. Ask for their input on subjects that should be covered and any gaps that exist in your current policy. Whenever changes are made, be sure to provide written copies to all employees and get a signed acknowledgment back from them, showing they have received the document.

Home on the Range

Any owner of a small business, regardless of its size, is unaware of all the things that take place when they aren't looking or aren't around. Having documentation for how tasks are to be done, who has the authority to approve expenditures, and who is responsible to follow up with customers, vendors, and subcontractors, for example, provides the guardrails for employee behavior. Documentation sets limits for what is appropriate.

Think about it this way: day-to-day business is like being on a ranch. The policies, rules, and procedures you have in place are like the fencing at the border of the ranch. Employees have the freedom to accomplish tasks, determine priorities, and so on within the boundaries, and they should be encouraged to think about the best way to get their assigned tasks completed. As long as they stay on the ranch, all is well. When they wander off the ranch—outside the fence—they are on their own and consequences are likely. Employees need and want to know where the boundaries are, without having to be told every detail of how to perform their job.

Business Procedures, Policies, and Practices

For questions about where to begin or which areas are most important to have documentation for, consider the following as a guide:

- Anywhere legal action has been brought or threatened against the company. This may involve areas such as employee policies, vendor and subcontractor agreements, and documentation regarding customer contracts, pricing, and scope of work.

- Areas where delivery of services to customers or internal processing is generating a high level of external or internal customer complaints, quality problems, and the need to redo work. Be sure to identify situations where inadequate employee training is the cause, as opposed to not having a clearly documented way of performing the job.

- All sources of cost overruns or reduced profitability that can be traced to not following a prescribed set of steps or reviews. This may include sourcing materials or subcontracted work from unapproved vendors as well as internal inefficiencies.

- Processes where employees have repeatedly asked for guidance on how something should be done or have complained or commented that they have received different instructions on the proper methods from different people.

The most urgent needs might not be within the operations function—those people and departments that produce and deliver your products and services. Inconsistency, poor quality, and lack of attention to detail related to internal processes such as timekeeping, bookkeeping, invoicing customers, paying suppliers and vendors, and employee policies can be equally damaging and costly not only to your business but to your ability to retain good people.

Continuous Improvement

An important aspect of a healthy organizational culture is a focus on continuous improvement—always seeking ways to get better, to improve in areas of efficiency, customer satisfaction, and quality. Documented processes and procedures form the basis for improvement. When a better way is found or new technology provides new solutions, the documented processes must be updated to reflect the changes. When all employees are then apprised of the changes, consistency is maintained along with reaping the benefits of the improved methods.

Creating a culture where employees are encouraged to always be thinking about new and better ways to perform work is an important part of motivating people and staying ahead of the competition. Focus is critical here! Don't work on improving many different aspects of your business at the same time. Prioritize. Start with areas where quality, cost, or customer satisfaction is a problem. Assign responsibility to a single employee for improving the process. Decide what metrics will be used to measure performance and capture the current baseline. After changes have been implemented, continue to track the metrics to verify that the performance has improved.

Tracking Performance

It is important to be able to track performance to measure the impact of changes you have made that are pertinent to the subject of policies, practices, and procedures. When using these or other key performance indicators to track performance improvement, be sure to measure your current performance, perhaps going back in time a year or two, to set a baseline. Then track the same metrics after you implement your changes to verify that you are achieving the intended results.

In your annual business planning process, include setting targets or goals for the coming year for the chosen metrics. Here are some examples:

Disciplinary Action—number of disciplinary actions (verbal or written warnings, suspensions, and terminations) completed in the past year.

Legal Action—number of occasions during the past 12 months where the lack of appropriate language in a written policy resulted in a lawsuit, grievance, or other legal action against the company.

Customer Satisfaction—average of all customer service ratings received over the past year.

CHAPTER 10

Positional Succession Planning

Succession planning is about long-term continuity in an organization and sustained profitable growth of the business. It is recognizing that changes will happen and people will leave the company, whether planned or unplanned. The foundation for coping successfully with staffing surprises is found in succession planning. Knowing that you cannot always predict when changes will take place, it is important to be as prepared as possible.

Succession planning is part of a risk management strategy aimed at minimizing a company's exposure to a skills shortage, especially in times of crisis such as the sudden departure of an owner, executive, or uniquely skilled employee.

While no single executive, manager, or employee is indispensable, some have extensive experience or specific knowledge that is critical to the business. It's up to business owners and leaders to develop the "bench strength"—the talent, skills, and experience—of others in the organization to prepare them to step in and succeed when openings occur.

Sometimes the Structure Is the Culprit

Having the ability to rapidly fill critical operations positions is always important, but in some cases the organization structure itself dramatically increases the need for bench strength behind key positions. Such was the case with a client we worked with a few years ago.

This client's project manager position had evolved to the point where they were not only responsible for managing jobs and meeting the schedule and profit goals but also accountable for driving leads through the insurance industry by developing relationships with brokers and adjusters who fed them work. Their compensation

---

(Continued)

(Continued)

model included bonuses based on profits generated. The position had evolved over time and because it resulted in profitable growth for the business, it was considered a viable model and not viewed as a potential threat.

The reality is that this structure did create a weakness for the business and exposed a critical need for succession. The project managers, not the company, "owned" the relationships with the insurance partners. When several of the project managers were recruited by a competitor, the jobs and their revenue followed. With the company having no plan in place for succession or alternate contacts for the insurance industry referral sources, revenue dropped quickly and significantly. A massive restructuring and downsizing followed.

We see similar succession weaknesses exposed in companies where key positions have no back-ups in place and potential successors have failed to be identified, let alone developed.

Effective succession planning provides many important benefits to an organization:

- Increased availability of capable individuals for management positions.

- Reduced risks from losing experienced company employees and leaders.

- Reduced costs for external searches and development of candidates to replace employees who leave.

- The creation of formal procedures to support the talent development process.

- The organization effectively copes with overall low levels of unemployment and talent scarcity in the industry.

- Improved capabilities in identifying skill gaps and training needs.

- Increased ability for the company to retain established knowledge, helping to better serve customers over an extended period of time.

- Boosted morale and retention by having invested in employees.

- Situations avoided where an individual employee can effectively hold an organization hostage because of their unique, critically needed skills and knowledge.

Succession planning is more than just a replacement planning process; it requires a comprehensive employee development system. The two most critical elements in a successful succession planning process are:

1. Identify potential successors for key positions.

2. Develop the successors based on knowledge of their needed capabilities and competencies.

Succession planning is not a short-term process. Effective development of suitable replacements for executive and management positions takes time. The most important component is an owner with a long-term vision and the commitment to continually invest in their people. Here's such an example.

Strong Long-Term Plan

A business owner came to us with a straightforward objective: "I only want to work two days a week." He had other goals in his life that he wanted to pursue, and he hired us to help him reach the point with his business where he could. As is the case with many businesses their size, the solution we recommended was to put a general manager in place to run the business. We began by defining the position and identifying the needed skills and experience. Internal candidates were identified, and development plans were implemented to grow their capabilities and expand their knowledge.

Within a year of the first person taking on the GM role, they left the business due to the relocation of their spouse. Because part of the long-term plan was to continue to groom successors for the GM and other management positions, one of the branch managers was ready and stepped in to take over.

(Continued)

(*Continued*)

> For various reasons, the position turned over four times in five years. Because a solid plan was in place, each time there was an existing employee who had been brought in or identified and developed with the intention that they would be prepared for the job.
>
> Like the NFL, MLB, or Division 1 college football teams who build their programs around being able to plug in new players when others graduate or leave for more money, it's about being able to "reload" your staff with people who are prepared to step into new roles. This process happens very quickly as opposed to a rebuilding process which implies that the recruiting, training, and preparation begin only when the vacancy arises.

As you can see, it's not just having the right people, but having a solid, long-term plan that leads to consistent succession for key positions.

Where to Start

A commitment to training is where succession planning starts. It begins with effective training for all employees for the roles they are in currently. It then moves to career planning where the interests and abilities of your people are identified and matched to the possibilities within the organization. This leads to development, which is preparing an employee for future positions and greater levels of responsibility. Finally, you're ready for replacement planning to identify possible replacements for key personnel.

Considerations for the Creation of Succession Plans

Effective succession plans are driven by more than simply listing names of current employees who may be candidates to fill a box on your organizational chart. Think longer term. Where is the business going? What services will be offered in the future? What geographic area will be served? Answers to these and other strategy questions lead to what the organizational structure will look like in the future and the skills and competencies that will be needed. If this is new to your organization, be sure to include the critical step of communicating about succession planning to everyone in the company. Tell them what it's about and how you will go about it.

Keep in mind that not all succession roles are intended to be permanent. Sometimes, it's simply a matter of having someone able to step in for short periods to cover illnesses, vacations, or family leave.

Take the important first step by identifying those who currently play a critical role in the success of your business. Then think about others who have unique skills, abilities or knowledge, and the experience that is key to the performance of your business and its ability to deliver specific services. These are the positions where being prepared for succession is most important.

It's after all this that the real work begins. Start by identifying internal candidates who have demonstrated that they have significant potential. You'll need to think about where they may be a likely fit in the future and what their personal goals are. Then define and execute training and development for each individual. This isn't a short-term project. It's a long-term commitment and requires consistent effort. Monitor each person's progress over time, adapt individual development plans as needed, and continually assess how prepared your company is to replace key positions on short notice.

There are several ways to approach the creation of succession plans. Regardless of choice, effective succession plans are based on having considered the following topics and issues:

- Identifying future service needs. Where is the company going in the future? What skills and competencies will be needed for success?

- Considering the current and future structure of the organization.

- Identifying key positions and competencies of internal leaders, managers, and employees. Maintaining up-to-date job descriptions that include skill and competency requirements, along with the ability to match needed talents to the tasks performed in any given job.

- Aligning and ensuring the consistency of existing practices—having standardized functional processes means performance, as defined by the expected outcomes, becomes easy to identify and observe.

- Defining the standards and metrics for how performance is measured and describing the expected results.

- Communicating the idea and reality of a succession planning program to the entire organization.

- Identifying and selecting internal candidates who have demonstrated high potential.

- Defining and implementing training and development activities for individuals who have been identified.

- Monitoring and evaluating progress.

- Planning for successful transitions by identifying the needed steps and how long they will take.

Identify Possible Successors

For each of the key critical positions identified, that position's manager is accountable to create a list of the one or two existing employees who are already prepared, or can be developed, to succeed the person in the job. The owner will have this responsibility for most or all of the management positions in the organization. This process should include an initial assessment of the areas where each successor needs to be developed.

In smaller companies, it is likely that a single employee may be on the list of possible successors for multiple positions. This is a good thing! Your high-performing employee should have the skills and willingness to learn that makes them a good candidate for more than one position, likely in more than one department of the organization.

It is also possible that no internal candidates exist for a critical management position or a more-technical role that requires unique skills, abilities, and experience. In these cases, responsibility must be assigned to begin the process of searching outside the organization for possible successors.

This doesn't necessarily mean that you need to go out and hire a successor now. Identifying external candidates means you can begin the process of learning more about them, meeting with them to understand their future aspirations, and exploring their level of interest in joining your company.

Development Plans

Preparing employees for key roles or positions of greater responsibility is an ongoing, long-term process. Leaders in the organization must be committed to driving the process, tracking progress, and continually evaluating the risks that are present. After possible successors and their development needs have been identified, the next step is to create individual development plans.

For each successor, create a list of the development needs you have determined. The responsible manager should consult with internal or external human resource experts for help in developing these lists. You won't be able to focus on all of a person's development needs right away, so plan to identify and address the most critical needs first.

The organization's leadership team should review succession candidates annually to track their development progress and confirm the positions for which they are being groomed. This can include a general "fire in the belly" assessment to determine if the candidate still has the drive to advance within the company.

For smaller organizations or companies where candidates are being considered for high-level positions, this could include cross-training in the various functional areas of the business. Doing so will give candidates a greater understanding of the work that is done in each area, along with first-hand experience of the tasks, frustrations, and challenges. This insight will serve them well as they transition into their new positions.

Refer to Chapter 11 on Professional Development for additional information on the process and tools for effective employee development.

Considerations

As you begin to move through the process of preparing successors in your organization, be sure to let those employees know, in private meetings, that you are preparing them for positions of increased responsibility. Be sure to explain that there are no guarantees and circumstances may change, but you see in them the potential for growth. Use opportunities such as vacations, family leave, or other temporary absences to give potential successors additional authority or responsibility. These situations will provide valuable experience for the employee and help your assessment of their potential and where development is needed.

While the owner may view this preparation as a prize or reward for the employee being tapped for advancement, this isn't always the case. Allow plenty of time for candid conversations to determine if this matches the direction the employee wants their career to progress.

Another factor to take into consideration is the employee's "flight risk." In other words, how likely are they to leave the company after you've invested the time to groom them into the new position? This doesn't need to be for business reasons. It could also be for personal, family, or health reasons.

Remember, when a person is tapped to replace a key individual, that employee will need replacing as well. Recognize talent gaps that may be created in those situations and take them into account in your hiring efforts.

Don't overlook successors for the owner! If the owner decides to retire or take advantage of another opportunity, it's critical that you've thought through the transition. Are there employees on board who have the potential to rise to that level? What can you be doing now to prepare them? While this is important in any organization, it's especially important in family businesses where the next generation of family members needs to be developed for senior leadership positions.

Tracking Performance

It is important to be able to track performance to measure the impact of changes you have made that are pertinent to the subject of positional succession planning. When using these or other key performance indicators to track performance improvement, be sure to measure your current performance, perhaps going back in time a year or two, to set a baseline. Then track the same metrics after you implement your changes to verify that you are achieving the intended results.

In your annual business planning process, include setting targets or goals for the coming year for the chosen metrics. Here are some examples:

Employee Development—number of current employees who have been identified as possible successors and have an active employee development plan in place.

Management Position Fill Rate—number of management positions that have been filled over the past year by an employee who was identified and developed as a succession candidate divided by the total number of management positions filled during the same period.

Turnover (annual)—number of employees leaving the organization during a 12-month period divided by the average actual number of employees during the same period.

CHAPTER 11

Professional Development

Developing the people in their organization is the most important commitment an owner will make to the company's ongoing success and growth. Regardless of where you are in the life cycle of your business, your needs regarding the skills, abilities, and potential of your people are constantly changing.

People who started out with you and have been highly valuable employees may no longer be a good fit for your larger, more complex business. Changing technology, markets, and service offerings mean new skills are needed. Growing organizations require professional managers, and people with strong technical skills may not successfully make that transition.

Development, which is different from training, means that employees are encouraged and given opportunities to take on new and increased responsibilities, are coached and mentored by those with greater experience, and are regularly involved in discussions regarding their goals and aspirations.

Employee development involves two key aspects:

1. Helping employees improve performance in their current role.

2. Preparing employees for positions of greater responsibility.

Training

Training employees is the most critical investment you will make in your business. For the following reasons, training must be the highest priority item in your annual budget or plan.

1. New employees must be taught how to do the work, how to complete the required documentation, and how they should interact

with customers, among other topics. Regardless of their level of prior experience, you need to train new employees on how things will be done in your business. Assuming people know how work is supposed to be done is a sure path to lower productivity and inconsistent quality.

2. Formal certifications may be required for specific types of work your company does. Achieving those certifications in a timely manner is important for technical reasons, such as understanding the how and why of the way work is done, and for marketing reasons. Customers expect that the people working for them have received appropriate training recognized by industry authorities.

The other factor here is consistency. When all employees receive the same training and clearly understand the processes you have in place, the services you provide will be the same regardless of who performs the work.

3. Acquiring additional skills and capabilities means your employees are more valuable to you and your company. The more functions they can perform, the more flexibility you have in manpower planning. This added value should translate into increased earnings. The addition of skills over time provides employees with the opportunity to progress through a career path of increased responsibilities and increased compensation. (Refer to the information on Position Ladder in Chapter 2 on Career Path Development for Your People.)

New Hire Training

Newly hired employees may come with previous experience, whether on-site experience for technicians or accounting experience for a bookkeeper. In any case, your responsibility is to be sure they understand how tasks are to be completed in your business.

The first step is to provide them with short but intense training for their specific position. This training comes after the orientation every new employee should go through that covers information applicable to all employees.

Position-Specific Technical Training

A specific, written training plan and schedule should exist for every position in the company. Some of the training is conducted in-house, and others include vendor-supplied resources such as videos, online learning modules, and in-class, hands-on training programs. Training programs may be linked to industry certifications for specific services.

Management Skills

As people move into supervisory and management positions, new sets of competencies should be required that are not specific to a department or function such as sales, operations, or finance. It is critical that the business provides highly effective training, either internally or through external resources, in areas such as these:

- Discipline
- Conducting effective meetings
- Business planning and creating goals and objectives
- Budgeting and cost management
- Performance management
- Time management
- Accountability
- Organization
- Decision making
- Emotional intelligence
- Motivation
- Safety
- Employee and communication styles (DiSC, Myers–Briggs, etc.)
- Conflict resolution
- Coaching for success
- Delegation and accountability
- Training and development
- Prioritization
- Collaboration
- Strategic thinking

Succession Planning

A key role of company owners and leaders is to maintain continuity in management and other critical positions within the company. Some personnel changes, like retirements, are planned and time is available to select and groom suitable replacements. One of leadership's responsibilities is to be sure the organization is as prepared as possible to deal with the need to fill any job opening that arises with a person both appropriate for the position and with a high probability of success. This should be done in a timely manner.

The process of preparing to do this is called succession planning. At its core is the responsibility of every manager within the organization, including owners, to have a short list of employees or people outside the organization who are best suited to replace them if needed. This pre-planning aims to avoid the frantic and less-than-well-thought-out, knee-jerk decisions that can result in response to unanticipated departures of employees, managers, and executives.

Refer to Chapter 10 on Positional Succession Planning for more information.

Individual Development Plans

Development is personal, meaning that it looks different for each individual. It's based on what skills and experience a person currently has and where they want to go. Managers within the organization must be accountable for tracking employee performance, providing timely feedback, and planning for growth in people's skills and abilities. Consistent, ongoing evaluation of employees and a commitment to developing their technical and functional skills is critical not only to improving the performance and supporting the growth of your business but also to retaining and providing motivation for your most valuable assets—your people.

Individual development plans should be created for employees as part of the performance management process. Remember that employee development is driven by two factors:

1. Improving performance in their current role.

2. Preparing them for positions of greater responsibility

The purpose of these plans is to assist in developing the technical, functional, and management skills of employees by identifying areas of need, drafting a plan for improvement, and tracking progress toward the improvement goals on a regular basis. The plans should be unique for each employee and focus on the few areas in most need of improvement.

To help you in creating development plans, refer to the **Employee Development Planner** template in the online Appendix.

As is suggested by author Bradford D. Smart, PhD, in his book *Topgrading*, we also recommend assessing an employee's competencies based on intellectual, personal, interpersonal, and technical categories. Each of these categories should then be separated into detailed competencies with examples provided. Specific skills that may be focused on within an individual plan could include:

- Judgment and decision making
- Creativity
- Adaptability and cost management
- Communication
- Technical competencies in areas such as finance, sales, software, and service-specific knowledge

- Integrity
- Organization and planning
- Customer focus
- Negotiating
- Delegating

The employee development process consists of the following steps:

1. From your list of professional and technical competencies, select no more than three that you believe are most critical to the individual employee's ongoing development or required improvement.

2. Enter each competency that has been identified as needing improvement on a separate employee development action plan form found at the end of the Employee Development Planner. Working with the employee, draft a development goal for each of the competencies and a specific time frame for accomplishing the goal.

3. Create a preliminary plan for achieving the goal, including training, seminars, workshops, reading, or other development tools with which you plan to assist the employee. A convenient way to think of this is with the 70-20-10 model, which speaks to most development needs coming from experience (70 percent), followed by learning from others (20 percent), followed by learning through formal means (10 percent).

4. Include a specific plan for periodic follow-up, review, and feedback to track progress over the course of time allotted for improvement.

5. Execute the plan and follow-ups, tracking performance and providing feedback to the employee. Make necessary adjustments to the development plan based on the effectiveness of the tools.

Mentoring

Mentoring, in simple terms, is a relationship in which a person with more experience or knowledge helps guide a person with less experience or knowledge. In a business organization, this is typically a long-term relationship focused on the growth and development of the person being mentored (the mentee).

Mentors should be people you want young or high-potential employees to learn from and emulate. Often mentors are in place to help others become better leaders.

What a mentor does:

- Takes a long-range view of the growth and development of the mentee.

- Helps the mentee to see the desired destination but does not give them a detailed map to get there.

- Shares stories of examples and events that helped them progress throughout their career.

- Offers encouragement and cheerleading but not how-to advice.

The mentee's responsibilities:

- Focus on being coachable and open to hearing feedback from the mentor, regardless of whether or not it is positive.

- Don't be afraid to ask for unvarnished advice or critiques. Practice skills as a good listener, take what is useable, and leave the rest.

- Provide structure for the relationship and specify initial career goals up front, such as learning specific procedures or processes or preparing for a promotion.

- Discuss how you can best measure together the success and effectiveness of the mentoring relationship.

- Make it a point to schedule conversations with the mentor and faithfully keep those appointments.

- Commit to specific steps in your developmental progress, discuss taking educated risks to support career development, and stay focused on personal goals. Keep track of discussions with the mentor and follow up on those during your meetings.

- Brainstorm for ways that you can help drive and maintain your relationship with the mentor. While the mentor invests their time to help you, you must also participate and actively pursue learning.

Ideas to Help You Succeed With a Mentor

Understanding the role of the mentor is a critical starting point for success in this relationship. Additional requirements include:

- Investing your time in seeking out a mentor with whom you feel a natural fit.

- Sharing your goals and fears openly.

- Not looking for the mentor to solve your short-term problems or do the work for you.

- Not expecting specific advice.

- Sharing where you are struggling or failing.

- Listening carefully and then researching and applying the mentor's guidance.

- Showing that you value the mentor's support.

- Not abusing the relationship by expecting "political" support in the organization.

Mentoring Models

There are a number of options for the type and structure of formal mentoring programs.

One-on-One Mentoring—the most common mentoring model, one-on-one mentoring matches one mentor with one mentee. Most people prefer this model because it allows both mentor and mentee to develop a personal relationship and provides individual support for the mentee. The availability of mentors is the only limitation.

Group Mentoring—group mentoring requires a mentor to work with four to six mentees at one time. The group meets once or twice a month to discuss various topics. Combining senior and peer mentoring, the mentor and peers help one another learn and develop appropriate skills and knowledge.

Group mentoring is limited by the difficulty of holding meetings on a regular basis for the entire group. It also lacks the personal relationship that most people prefer in mentoring. For this reason, it is often combined with the one-on-one model. For example, some organizations provide each mentee with a specific mentor. In addition, the organization offers periodic meetings in which a senior executive meets with all the mentors and mentees, who then share their knowledge and expertise.

Resource-Based Mentoring—resource-based mentoring offers some of the same features as one-on-one mentoring. The main difference is that mentors and mentees are not interviewed and matched by a mentoring program manager. Instead, mentors agree to add their names to a list of available mentors from which a mentee can choose. It is up to the mentee to initiate the process by asking one of the volunteer mentors for assistance.

Executive Mentoring—this top-down model may be the most effective way to create a mentoring culture and cultivate skills and knowledge throughout an organization. It is also an effective succession-planning tool because it prevents the knowledge "brain drain" that would otherwise take place when senior managers retire.

Implementing a Mentoring Program

When deciding to implement mentoring within your organization, use the following steps to set goals, define the process to be used, and prepare to measure the effectiveness of the program.

1. **Establish goals for the mentoring program.**

   - Retain and grow existing talent.

   - Expand leadership skills.

   - Increase "bench strength" for management positions.

   - Support succession planning.

2. **Identify the selection criteria for mentors and mentees.**

   - Include those who are eager, committed, and willing to do the work that will lead to transformation.

   - Define the qualifications for junior and veteran talent, such as years of experience, specific skills, and so on.

3. **Define other components of the program.**

   - How often pairs (mentor and mentee) are expected to meet.

   - How many people will participate in the pilot or initial rollout of the program.

   - What role technology will play.

   - What type of handout will be created to give all program details to the participants.

4. **Recruit and interview potential candidates**.

- Communicate using methods you are sure will reach the target employees.

- Provide a specific point of contact for their responses.

- Develop selection criteria to be used when interviewing candidates.

5. **Match participants based on the following (assuming you are using a one-on-one model)**.

- Compatibility, but never put an employee with their direct supervisor

- Employee goals that fit with the veteran's experience

- Communication styles

- Understanding the challenges mentees face and what they are expecting from the experience

6. **Evaluate program results**.

- Solicit feedback from all participants.

- Conduct short exit interviews with a prepared list of questions.

- Determine if the mentoring model was effective and why or why not.

- Find out how many of the participants were satisfied with their match.

7. **Next steps**.

- Define and implement necessary changes to the model.

- Expand the program as needed.

Tracking Performance

It is important to be able to track performance to measure the impact of changes you have made that are pertinent to the subject of professional development. When using these or other key performance indicators to track performance improvement, be sure to measure your current performance, perhaps going back in time a year or two, to set a baseline. Then track the same metrics after you implement your changes to verify that you are achieving the intended results.

In your annual business planning process, include setting targets or goals for the coming year for the chosen metrics. Here are some examples:

Professional Development Spend—total amount spent on employee professional development during the past 12 months divided by total revenue over the same period.

Training/Development Hours—sum of training hours for all employees during the previous year divided by the total number of employees.

Employee Development—number of employees who have an active employee development plan in place.

Promotions—number of employees who have been promoted or achieved a position of greater responsibility during the previous year.

Mentoring—number of employees who are involved in a mentoring relationship with a designated, trained mentor.

CHAPTER 12

Purposefulness of Employment

There is a generational component to recruiting and hiring. Rather than simply earning a paycheck, employees are looking for meaning in the work they do and the careers they choose.

People who own a business or work in service industries do so, at least in part, because of the opportunity to help and serve others. Whether it is part of your business's stated mission or not, it's at the heart of what you do. Don't neglect the opportunity to tout this deeper purpose or to state that your mission is driven by helping others.

As long as it is authentic and not a thinly veiled attempt to lure people to your company based on posing as "good people," letting others know about your focus on helping those in need within your community is a good idea.

A Worthy Cause

Who would have guessed that a 10-year-old organization would grow to over 120,000 volunteers doing back-breaking, dangerous work around the world to provide relief to people affected by natural disasters? Yet that's exactly what Jake Wood and William McNulty did when they founded Team Rubicon. That's the power of a compelling mission!

Team Rubicon isn't alone in this area. Consider all the nonprofit organizations, large and small, local and international, whose missions involve performing social services. These organizations attract highly talented people not because of their lavish pay or benefits, but because their missions speak to the hearts of their workers.

You don't have to be a Team Rubicon or a nonprofit organization to have talented people attracted to the purpose of your company. Many of the organizations VMA has worked with over the years have had missions (frequently unpromoted) just as compelling as that of Team Rubicon. Whether it's raising tens of thousands of dollars to provide shoes for people in impoverished areas, assembling and donating bicycles to underprivileged children, or establishing a nonprofit arm of their company to serve their local community, workers are attracted to these companies.

Employee Motivation

Whether as a career choice or in searching for employment, people may be attracted to work in an industry or for a business whose purpose or focus is helping others. Specifically, those born in the period between 1980 and the mid-1990s, referred to as millennials, are more likely to choose careers where they feel they are serving the greater good.

If your organization's mission and vision build on this, be sure to review and discuss them during the recruiting process. Explain to candidates how your people live your values and address the needs of others in all you do.

Community Involvement

The benefits of your business to the communities where you and your people work and live go beyond paying wages and taxes and buying from local suppliers. Your role as a business owner extends outside of the organization itself. You have an obligation to contribute to the greater wellbeing of the communities you serve.

Whether in the form of the owner's personal time or encouraging and permitting your people to become actively engaged in organizations that serve the community, it is important that you support and give back through time and resources.

This commitment produces benefits for your business as well. Hiring candidates should be aware of your people's involvement and your commitment to serve those around you, which will make you a more desirable employer.

Relationships built and developed through volunteering and community service will extend to your business and customer referrals.

Charitable Causes

In addition to general community service and support, many business owners have a personal tie to a particular charitable organization, cause, or condition. Being public about your support should not be feared as being viewed as egocentric or boasting.

For example, you being recognized as the local organizer of the annual St. Baldrick's fundraiser to support the fight against cancer, while driven by a personal experience, may enhance the opinion people have of your organization.

Tracking Performance

It is important to be able to track performance to measure the impact of changes you have made that are pertinent to the subject of purposefulness of employment. When using these or other key performance indicators to track performance improvement, be sure to measure your current performance, perhaps going back in time a year or two, to set a baseline. Then track the same metrics after you implement your changes to verify that you are achieving the intended results.

In your annual business planning process, include setting targets or goals for the coming year for the chosen metrics. Here are some examples:

Contributions—sum of all contributions to charitable and community organizations over the past year divided by total revenue for the same period.

Volunteering—total number of hours company employees invested in community and charitable organizations and events during the past year.

Community Support—number of hours the business owner or CEO invested in community and charitable causes during the past year.

CHAPTER 13

Recruiting and Employment Promotion

The process of effectively hiring the right employees begins with attitude. The attitude that your success depends on the quality and effectiveness of the people you hire. The attitude that you and your people understand the core values upon which the company was built and that you hold your people accountable to those values. The attitude that you will not settle for hiring a candidate you think will be just okay in the job. The attitude that you will hire only "A" players—those who fit with the culture you have established within your organization and who have a high probability of succeeding in their position.

Successful organizations are always looking for the right people. Rather than simply hiring to fill an existing vacancy, they are able and willing to hire when the right person comes along. This doesn't imply that you hire indiscriminately, resulting in gross overstaffing. It means that you aren't only considering current needs but are keeping in mind future growth, thinking about succession planning for key positions, and the ability to upgrade personnel where improvement is needed.

This philosophy should not be interpreted as being at odds with a promote-from-within strategy. Continued development of existing personnel should always be a priority and having employees reach their full potential is the goal. However, there will be situations where additional capacity is required, promotion to support expansion or succession creates a vacancy that cannot be filled, or skills and experience are needed that don't exist within the organization.

A healthy approach to recruiting and hiring means you continue through the process until you find the right person. Decisions aren't rushed. You don't settle for candidates who are "good enough" because of a perceived sense of urgency. The phrase "hire slow" is fitting.

To learn more, the book *The Ideal Team Player: How to Recognize and Cultivate the Three Essential Virtues* by Patrick Lencioni is suggested.

Employment Promotion

The terminology of employment promotion means that company owners and leaders recognize that their ability to staff the organization with top-level talent is a 24-hours-a-day, 365-days-a-year effort. Customers, vendors, partners, and members of employees' personal networks understand that we are always looking for great people. Continuous efforts are made to create and enhance relationships with those in areas such as education, hospitality, and other businesses where leaders interact with people they may recognize as being a potential good fit for our company.

Leaders and employees alike regularly talk about the culture within the organization, the fact that it is a great place to work, and that we offer the opportunity for a career not simply a job. Members of the leadership team see part of their responsibility being to inform the public about our industry, the services we provide, the customers we serve, and the opportunities we offer in jobs, wages, benefits, and training and development.

The point is that there will be times when there may not be a specific position that needs to be filled, but it is recognized that the business can only grow and improve to a level that can be supported by its people.

Employment Promotion Activities

Some of the activities covered under the umbrella of employment promotion include, but are not limited to, the following:

- All managers carry preprinted cards designed to be presented to service providers who have shown strong customer focus and a drive to satisfy. The cards include your company name and personal contact information along with a message like: "You have really impressed me with your focus on customer service. You are the kind of person I (we) want in our organization. Please contact me if you are interested in exploring the opportunities we have to offer."

- All managers regularly remind people in their personal network that you are always looking for people who have the drive to grow and succeed, are customer focused, and may be looking for something better than their current position.

- Assign responsibility for building and maintaining relationships with educators who have contact with high school and postsecondary students. Make sure they know the types of work you do, the positions you have, and the characteristics you desire. Contact them periodically to ask about current students or recent graduates they would recommend.

- Develop and market internships or project opportunities where students can work in your business for a short period on tasks of limited scope. This provides you with exposure to potential employees with the added benefit of seeing how they interact and fit with your existing employees.

- Create and maintain a Careers or Open Positions page on your company website. This page should contain information on the type of people you are looking for, career opportunities that are available within the organization, and specific positions you are currently looking to fill.

- All management and leadership team members leverage opportunities to speak to groups within the community to emphasize your continual search for the right people who are looking for an opportunity to work in an environment like yours.

- Implement an employee referral incentive. Current employees referring candidates who are hired and remain with the company for a defined period are provided an economic incentive.

Leadership

The ability to make good decisions about people is one of the last reliable sources of competitive advantage. Understanding human nature means we tend to attract and hire people like us—people of the same faith, customs, values, and beliefs; similar socio-economic strata; familiar financial expectations and cultural interests; and those close to us in age with similar life experiences. Enlightened leaders recognize the value of diversity and of different perspectives and approaches to solving problems. They are committed to maintaining a culture where diversity is valued and thrives.

The other element that may be driven by our nature is hiring people who are equal to us when it comes to competency. When we recognize our personal limitations and the impact they have on taking our business to the vision we created, two things are clear:

1. Continually increasing our personal competence is necessary to attract employees with higher levels of competencies.

2. Getting past the mindset that we need to be the smartest person in the room.

A good starting point to overcoming these natural tendencies is to perform a self-examination by thinking how you've felt when a highly competent person applied for a position in your organization. Was it uncomfortable? Did you find yourself looking hard for any shortcomings?

Although this may be a natural first response when feeling a bit inadequate, strong leaders recognize that having top-level talent means having people who are more knowledgeable than they are. They realize this is a good thing! Their company will be able to grow even stronger than if it was relying only on them.

Once you've come to the realization that highly competent people are exactly who you want to attract to your company, it's time for even more introspection.

Just as we ask tough questions during interviews in an effort to make the right hiring decisions, talented employment candidates want to be sure they're also making the right career decision when hiring into your company.

By candidly considering a few hardball questions before recruiting new hires, you might gain valuable insights into just how attractive your company will be to highly talented candidates. Ask yourself how well you'd score if those being interviewed were to turn around and ask you the following questions:

- If I had the chance to speak privately with three of your current employees, how would they describe you as a business leader and as a person?

- On a professional level, how do you manage your people and the business?

- How do you conduct yourself, what is your management style?

- What do you stand for, even in difficult situations?

- What have you done in the last three months to recognize outstanding performance by one of your people or teams?

- What areas of professional growth are you, yourself, working on right now?

- Do you invest time and money in your own professional growth or has your thinking and management style calcified into "the way we've always done things"?

- Are the work issues that keep you up at night now any different from those that kept you up at night a year ago?

- If you won the lottery tomorrow, would you close the business?

Asking tough questions about yourself and your businesses isn't easy, but with the employment market as competitive as it is, giving your company an honest evaluation based on hardball questions like these before you start recruiting can help you not only attract the best employees but keep them.

Position Descriptions

Complete, accurate, and up-to-date written position descriptions—also called job descriptions—must exist for every position in the company. They are the starting point for any hiring that takes place and answer many questions candidates may have about the job and its principal responsibilities, required skills, knowledge, and experience.

Position descriptions should include the following:

- Job title, department, status (exempt or nonexempt), position type (part-time, full-time, etc.), and reporting structure

- Position summary/purpose

- Duties and responsibilities

- Decision rights and authority

- Working relationships and scope

- Performance competencies

- Qualifications (knowledge, skills, and abilities)

- Physical demands

- Working conditions

- Position acknowledgment and signature area

A template, including explanations for the content of each section, can be found in the online Appendix under **Job Description Content**.

Recruiting Scope

Success in hiring the most competent people, especially in a tight labor environment, relies on casting a wide net for candidates. The North American workforce is growing more slowly than the demand for workers, especially in the service sector. Multiple sources, including the following, should be used when recruiting for all positions:

- The Internet

- Referrals—internal and external

- Professional and social networking sites

- Job fairs

- Internal promotion

- Colleges and trade schools

- Newspapers and publications

- Employee temporary agencies

Recruiting Tactics

In addition to the in-person, online, social media, and print outlets where employment ads should be placed, consider the following tactics to narrow your focus and increase the likelihood of reaching valuable candidates.

- Task every supervisor and manager in the organization with maintaining a list of internal candidates who are potential successors for every position under their leadership, including their own.

- Understand the outside interests of your high-performing employees. Where you find some consistency among them, reach out to those organizations, activities, clubs, and so on to post ads or make them aware of your hiring needs.

- Gather input from hiring candidates and other job seekers on the sources they rely on for quality job postings, regardless of their position or industry.

- Analyze the responses to your job postings—both quality and quantity—by source. Compare fees and restrictions to continually update the sites and publications you use.

- Partner with school placement services to not only reach current students but to provide access to recent graduates and to seek speaking opportunities at the schools whenever possible, even though this is outside the wheelhouse of many business owners.

- Use trustworthy recruiters and headhunters.

Hiring Process

Consistently effective hiring, once the position to be filled has been defined, requires having in place the process steps outlined below and following them every time you hire a new person.

1. Advertising

2. Screening

3. Sending a questionnaire

4. Interviewing

5. Completing background checks

6. Testing

7. Presenting an offer of employment

While the process steps may be modified somewhat based on the position to be filled, it is critical that the steps be completed in order and in a timely fashion.

Refer to the **Employee Selection and Hiring Guidelines** document in the online Appendix.

Screening Candidates

Each step in the recruiting and hiring process is about deciding which candidates should advance to the next step. This funnel method means there are fewer and fewer people being considered as you move through the process. Screening the applications or resumés generated by your employment ads or network connections is the first step.

At this point, all you typically know about the candidate comes from the information on their application or resumé. Your goal is to identify the people you believe can be successful in the position that needs to be filled. Keep in mind that those who are most likely to fit into the culture of your organization and succeed in the position aren't necessarily those with the most experience in a similar job. In order to successfully filter out those with the highest likelihood of success, focus on the following key areas:

- The sequence of positions held, noting any gaps in employment, looking for progression in the level of responsibility and growth of skills. You want to see career or job progression in their work history. Having a gap in employment along with career progression is not necessarily something of concern and may be explained during the next phase of the process. Multiple gaps in employment could be a factor that indicates a lower likelihood of success.

- The rate of change in jobs and employers, meaning the length of time in each position. If you see frequent job changes within the same industry or industries that require transferable skills, this may be explained as career progression or searching for the right employer and should be noted as something to discuss in the next phase of the process. Frequently changing jobs within multiple industries or without a connection in the skills required may indicate a likelihood of continued job movement.

- Measurable indicators of achievement and success.

For those candidates you decide to move to the next step in the process, make notes of questions you will pursue in the questionnaire or interview phase, based on the content in their application or resumé.

Those involved in the hiring process are then challenged with the daunting task of evaluating each candidate against the established criteria. The most challenging part is getting through the rehearsed answers and responses they learned through online research to uncover who the candidates really are as people. Question every answer and run them through a rigorous logic test. Do the answers make logical sense?

Candidate Characteristics and Experience

The required characteristics should relate back to your staffing priorities and the position requirements. Think about the characteristics you're looking for in the ideal person for the job. As you're listing these characteristics, consider how the specific job will be performed when the person possesses them.

Start by creating a list of the six to eight "must have" characteristics and experiences required for the specific position. Then create a second list of those that are "preferred." Here are a few examples for use with a sales position.

Must Have	Preferred
Integrity Iron clad. Does not cut corners. Puts the company's interests above self. Earns trust of co-workers; is intellectually honest; does not play games.	**Professional Development Mindset** Takes initiative to develop own professional skills.
Communication—Oral Strong communication one on one and in small and large groups. "Quick on feet."	**Experience** In your industry.
Communication—Written Writes clear, precise, well-organized letters, emails, and proposals. Uses appropriate vocabulary and has impeccable grammar and word usage.	**Team Player** Reaches out to peers to tear down walls. Has a reputation for leading peers toward support of what's best for the company. Establishes collaborative relationships with peers.

Candidate Evaluation Criteria

In preparation for reviewing responses to employment ads and other lead-generation activities, it is important to establish standards for how the candidates will be evaluated at each step in the hiring process.

Before hiring begins, the hiring manager and HR representative should work together to establish the criteria to be rated at each step.

1. Cover letter and resumé

2. Application

3. Questionnaire (when applicable)

4. Phone interview

5. First interview

6. Skills assessment (when applicable)

7. Second interview

Application and Resumé Review

Applications are fairly straightforward. You are looking at each candidate's relatively recent job and compensation history.

Resumés are more detailed and ought to provide more useful information regarding employers, positions, and results. Remember these basic facts.

- Many people lie, or at least embellish, on their resumé.

- This is as good as it gets. A candidate's resumé is likely to be the product of a significant investment of their time and has also potentially been reviewed by someone skilled in the areas of structure, grammar, and overall appearance. If the document contains errors, typos, and other flaws, just imagine what this person's output will look like when they're in a hurry!

You are trying to achieve three things when reviewing an applicant's resumé or application.

1. Become familiar with the person's credentials, background, and qualifications as they relate to the responsibilities and requirements of the job.

2. Determine if they should be considered as a candidate for the position; should they move to the next step in the process?

3. Identify areas where you want to gather additional information through the questionnaire or interview process.

A technique that many managers find useful when assessing a group of candidates for a position is to give a letter grade—A, B, or C—to each resumé. First, it serves to provide a way to rank candidates from best to least impressive. Second, and perhaps more important, if multiple managers are reviewing the resumés, those candidates who received different letter grades from the reviewers should then be discussed to determine what drove the varying assessments. Different perspectives or experiences of the reviewing managers may cause candidates to be considered who may otherwise have been passed over.

Here are the steps to follow for a thorough review and assessment of a candidate's resumé.

1. **Scan the overall appearance of the resumé.** Is it easily readable? Is it organized in a logical way?

2. **Look for blanks and omissions.** Do you feel like you have a complete picture of the person's work history? Are there time periods between school and work that are unaccounted for?

3. **Review work history and note any gaps in time between jobs.** Even within the same employer, are there time periods where it is not clear what position they held?

4. **Consider any overlaps in jobs.**

5. **Look for inconsistencies.** Look at the progression of positions and titles over time. Is the person growing and moving into jobs with more responsibility? Are the responsibilities and achievements shown consistent with the job title?

6. **Consider the frequency of job changes.** How many job and employer changes have there been and what explanations are provided for them?

7. **Be objective when evaluating salary requirements.** Does their stated compensation make sense relative to the responsibilities of the job?

8. **Carefully review reasons for leaving previous jobs.** Is there any indication that they did not perform or did not fit the culture of an organization, or is the reason always someone else's fault?

9. **Prepare questions about past job duties and responsibilities that are not clearly described.** Ask the questions that the resumé presents. Ask about performance: how it was measured and what they achieved. When they show extraordinary results or achievements, ask

how they did it. What was their role in making it happen? Were others responsible for the outcome, too?

Always look for red flags. Sometimes there are things in people's resumés that just don't fit and don't make sense with the rest of the story. Gaps in time or changes in responsibilities that clearly signal a demotion.

Questionnaire

The next step in the hiring process is to present the applicants with a series of questions in written form. The questions you use will be driven by the position to be filled and the information provided, or omitted, on their resumé or application. The purpose is to gather more information on how the individuals interpret and respond to open-ended questions, how they communicate in writing, and their attention to detail (spelling, punctuation, grammar, and so on). This process will be handled differently depending on the position being filled.

- For nonmanagement positions, give the questions to the candidates, printed on your company letterhead, with the employment application.

- For management, business development, and other professional positions (project managers, estimators, and so on) email questions to the selected candidates. Be sure to include a cover letter with specific instructions on how to reply and the expected timing.

When developing questionnaire content, focus on gathering additional insight into the candidate in these critical areas.

- **Research and commitment to the job-hunting process.** How much effort have they put into understanding your company—who you are and what you do?

- **Planning and goal setting.** In both their personal life and professional life, how effectively do they set goals and go about achieving them?

- **Teamwork and interpersonal style.** Do they appreciate working with others? How do they deal with personalities unlike their own? What attributes do they prefer their superior to have?

- **Technical competence.** What experience do they have performing specific tasks and working with tools like software programs that will be needed in the position?

- **Experience working in a small business.** Understand that those coming from a background of working in a large company or corporate environment may offer useful skills and abilities but may find challenges in working in a smaller organization.

- **Self-view and priorities.** How do they view their current position? What do they see as their most important responsibilities? How do they describe their work style?

Evaluating a completed questionnaire, when applicable, should be considered a vital step in the hiring process. A candidate's willingness to complete the questionnaire and the quality of their responses should help to quickly identify serious contenders. When reviewing, focus on these items in addition to the actual information conveyed in the answers:

- The depth and thoroughness of the person's thought processes and responses.

- The degree to which they have set goals for themselves and see the position as a step on the way.

- Their ability to express their thoughts and ideas clearly and concisely.

- Their "soft" skills such as personality, tolerance for challenging behaviors, and work style.

- Their attention to detail: grammar, spelling, and punctuation.

In terms of assessing a person's ability to think through a question, formulate their response, and present the response in an organized, concise, and thorough manner, the questionnaire offers a shorter time frame than the resumé but should allow for complete, logical, and grammatically correct responses.

Reading through responses to "soft skills" questions should provide enough insight into the person to support an initial assessment as to whether they would be a good fit with your organization.

Interviews

Hiring Rule #1: **Never** conduct an interview without first reviewing an applicant's resumé or application.

Phone Interview

In most cases, you will have gotten to this point in the process without having met face-to-face or spoken with those you are considering. The purpose of a phone interview is to hear the applicant talk, get a sense for how they think on their feet when presented with a question, and discern how well they can put their thoughts together quickly and express them clearly.

Use the following as a guide to prepare, execute, and assess each candidate's phone interview.

- Spend no longer than 15 minutes on the phone interview.

- Select a few questions based on their resumé, application, or questionnaire responses to ask during the phone interview.

- Ask open-ended questions that will require them to formulate a response and respond immediately.

- Determine if what you hear on the phone is consistent with what you've seen on paper.

- Introduce yourself, including your title, and let the candidate know that you are the person responsible for the hiring decision. Tell them that this is the next step in your hiring process.

- Listen to them talk. Assess their level of energy. You can hear their level of energy, excitement, or calmness over the phone.

- Evaluate how effectively they put together answers and express them on the spot.

If you are not impressed, thank the candidate for their time and let them know they will be hearing from you shortly. Send them an email the following day stating that you have decided to pursue other candidates you feel are a better fit with the position, then wish them well in their job search. For those you want to have proceed to a face-to-face interview, you can do either of the following:

- Tell the candidate while you are on the phone that you would like to arrange for them to come in for an interview. Let them know that someone (administration or HR department) will be contacting them to set up a time.

- Let the candidate know that someone will be in touch with them within 24 hours to discuss the next step in the process.

In-Person Interview

Based on the information you have on their background and their responses to the questions from the questionnaire or phone interview, every candidate who makes it to this point in the process should be capable of effectively performing the job being filled. The goal of the interview step is to determine the best candidate and to hire an "A" player.

Hiring Rule #2: **Never** hire a candidate without having at least two interviews with them.

Resist the temptation to break this rule when you are exhausted, overwhelmed, or when you think you've found the perfect candidate who doesn't "require" a second interview.

When you have decided to move to the in-person interview, you should have three goals in mind:

1. Develop an accurate picture of the job for which you are hiring and communicate it to every applicant.

2. Collect enough information on the candidate to make an informed decision.

3. Produce a positive and accurate picture of the company that will, hopefully, impress them and help them decide they want to work for you.

Face-to-Face Interview Preparation

Interviewing options include one-on-one and panel formats. Panel interviews include two or three interviewers with the candidate. The benefit of this format is that interviewers can compare their assessments, having all heard the same questions and responses. Having more than three interviewers at one time potentially creates a more threatening environment for the candidate.

Your building, office area, and your people should project a professional image. Remember that this process is not just about whether you like the candidate, but about selling your company to them. The interviewing area should be private and comfortable.

Preparing for face-to-face interviews includes the following steps.

1. Decide who within your organization will interview the candidate and what format will be used. The immediate supervisor (hiring manager) for the position being filled must interview each candidate and no hiring decision should be made without their consent. It is recommended that a peer or someone the person will be working with should also be included.

2. Produce a set of questions that must be covered during the interviews.

3. Be sure that all interviewers are briefed on the legal considerations of interviewing.

4. Instruct all interviewers on how, where, and when to provide their feedback on each candidate.

Here are some tips for successful interviewing.

- Allow sufficient time for the interview.

- Keep an open mind.

- They (candidates) talk; you listen (silence can be powerful).

- Be attentive.

- Remember that the candidates will never look better than they do today.

- Observe their body language.

- Take notes.

- Listen for how many questions they are asking about the job.

- Probe incomplete answers.

- Get others involved in the process.

- Test for character.

- When it comes to the legality of a question, if in doubt, leave it out.

As a final thought, be sure to solicit input from the person who greets the candidates when they enter your facility, even if they are not included in the formal interviewing process. Their assessment of the person's demeanor and how they were treated and shown respect (or not) is valuable input.

Interview Questions

Interview questions should be open-ended, meaning they cannot be answered with a simple "yes" or "no" response. This is intentional. It forces the candidate to talk and provide more explanation with their answers. Interview questions, typically 12 to 15, should also be determined in advance, based on several sources.

1. **Information from the applicant's resumé or application**. Inquire about missing information and gaps in employment and clarify previous responsibilities and accomplishments.

2. **Their responses to the written questionnaire**. Clarify the meaning and ask for more detail or background. Their replies

can provide opportunities for you to say, "Tell me more about that."

3. **Questions designed to assess personal characteristics**. Refer to the required characteristics and skills document for the position. Prepare questions that will provide insight into the critical characteristics of the job.

For those questions focused on assessing certain characteristics, here are some examples, based on the skill or characteristic you are evaluating.

General Questions

1. What are your strengths and weaknesses?

2. Why did you leave your last job?

3. Why should we hire you?

4. What is most important to you in a job?

5. What questions do you have for me?

Problem Solving

1. What is the most creative work-related idea that you have had?

2. Describe a difficult problem you faced and solved.

3. What approach to problem solving works best for you?

4. Describe something that you "made" as a result of a problem.

Questions About Motivation

1. What have you done that shows initiative?

2. What are some of your career objectives that have been met?

3. How do you measure success?

4. What rewards mean the most to you?

5. What types of projects do you get excited about?

Working With Others

1. What kind of people do you like to work with?

2. Tell me about a conflict you had with a fellow worker. How was it resolved?

3. How would you describe your management/leadership style?

4. How do others see you?

5. What would your previous boss tell us about you?

6. What three words describe you?

Integrity Indicators

1. Tell me about a time when you were not honest.

2. How would you react if you were asked to do something unethical?

3. If you saw a co-worker doing something dishonest, what would you do?

When it comes to interview questions, they must always be work-related. Legally, you cannot ask any questions that are personal in nature. The best rule to follow is if you are in doubt, leave it out!

Interview Debrief

As soon as possible after the conclusion of the interview, meet with all who participated to gather feedback and get their assessments. Determine if there is a consensus on the status of the candidate. If not, document the areas of concern and address them in the follow-up interview.

At this point in the process, you will ideally have two or three candidates you believe can be successful in the position. They should be scheduled for second interviews with the appropriate people in your organization.

If there is consensus among those who participated in the first interview that a candidate is strong, schedule a second interview before they leave the premises. This will convey to the candidate that they are being seriously considered and should cause them to wait until after their second interview with your organization to make comparisons with other opportunities they may have.

After the second interview, the candidates—two or three at the most—who are deemed to be viable contenders for the position will move to the next step in the process, which is reference checks.

Testing

For some positions, it is advisable to conduct testing of a candidate's abilities when doing so can be done in a timely manner. Such testing is aimed at verifying knowledge and capabilities with software; specific job functions such as estimating, bookkeeping, and treatment protocols; or understanding of metrics and reports used in the management of the business.

Examples of appropriate testing may include:

- Administrative positions are asked to duplicate a printed copy of a Word document.

- Testing for Excel spreadsheet capability is done by having the applicant create a spreadsheet with specific functionality by following a set of written instructions.

- Estimator candidates are asked to review photos of a room and a written estimate to identify missing line items.

- Bookkeeping applicants are asked to match expense receipts with a defined chart of accounts.

Reviewing and evaluating the test results should be done by the same person, as defined in advance, for all applicants. Results should be completed in a timely manner, documented, and communicated to the hiring manager.

Candidate Follow-Up

All candidates who go through the interview process but are not recommended for hiring should receive an email from the hiring manager, owner, or CEO letting them know that the company has decided to move forward with another candidate. Wish them well in their search and career.

If multiple candidates went through the final reference, background check, and testing steps, those not receiving an offer of employment should receive a phone call from the designated person (manager, CEO, or owner) advising them of your decision. These conversations should be very positive in tone, thanking them for their interest in your company and wishing them well in their future endeavors.

These conversations should be documented as to the date, time, originator, and content of the call. Avoid providing any specifics regarding the reasons other candidates were considered to be a better fit for the position.

Offer of Employment

When all the inputs have been reviewed and the best candidate identified, move quickly to create and communicate a formal offer of employment. You should contact the candidate by phone with a verbal offer, letting them know that a written offer is being sent.

This step should never be taken lightly, but once the decision is made, it should be executed in a timely manner to secure the candidate's commitment.

The offer letter should indicate that it is valid after successful completion of a background check. You can have candidates fill out an application that contains a signed waiver to conduct the background check should the offer be extended, but no checks (background, credit, driving, and so on) can be done before an official offer is made. Additionally, checks should only be done on the candidate being extended the offer. Doing any type of check before the offer can lead to a host of potential lawsuits.

Refer to the online Appendix documents **Offer of Employment** and **Conditional Offer of Employment** for more information and a sample of each.

Background Checks

A background check should always be conducted after extending an offer of employment. Three steps are critical:

1. Consider legal guidelines.

2. Establish a background-check policy for your company.

3. Secure a reputable vendor.

For a form you can use, refer to the online Appendix document **Background Check and Release**.

Tracking Performance

It is important to be able to track performance to measure the impact of changes you have made that are pertinent to the subject of recruiting and employment promotion. When using these or other key performance indicators to track performance improvement, be sure to measure your current performance, perhaps going back in time a year or two, to set a baseline. Then track the same metrics after you implement your changes to verify that you are achieving the intended results.

In your annual business planning process, include setting targets or goals for the coming year for the chosen metrics. Here are some examples:

Turnover (annual)—number of employees who leave the organization over the course of a year expressed as a percentage of total number of employees at year end.

Cost Per Hire—total cost including monetary costs, people's time in assessments, interviews, etc., and testing, background checks, and drug tests.

Job Posting—number of viable candidates received by ad/posting source, by position. This data will help to eliminate recruiting sources that aren't generating responses from candidates we are trying to reach.

CHAPTER 14

Trade Promotion

Your ability to consistently attract qualified candidates to your business will be greatly enhanced if you invest the time in exposing your company and your people to the community around you. Your brand will be recognized as a name that not only employs local people but is actively involved in supporting the places where you live and work.

Establishing reliable sources for properly trained candidates who can feed your business for years to come is a two-way street. It means getting out of your comfort zone, reaching out to schools and training program operators in your area, and beginning a dialogue on how you can help each other.

Partnering With Educational Institutions

In a previous career, one of our VMA advisors ran the Pittsburgh, PA branch of a large, national restoration company. Their demand for trade labor (carpenters, painters, drywallers, and so on) varied significantly, as it was driven by the jobs they landed. The corporate view was that this labor was necessary, but they had no particular strategy in place for how to find the right people. Turnover was high. Recruiting was hit or miss. The current address that one applicant included on their documentation turned out to be the county jail— and no, he was not employed there!

The solution came from a straightforward idea—develop a relationship with a local technical school that offered programs in some of the trades in which the company would have a consistent and ongoing need. Step one was reaching out to the school's administration and contacting the appropriate people. The company then offered to provide input and feedback on their curriculum and the skills the company was looking for, along with career opportunities

---

(Continued)

(Continued)

in the restoration industry. The reception was warm and the relationship was formed.

- The branch manager would attend all monthly school board meetings.

- Employer input was expected on any topics the board was discussing.

- Feedback was requested on curriculum content and future programs.

- The branch manager was afforded the opportunity to speak to students two to three times per year about career opportunities.

- Unused materials from the restoration company's jobs were donated to the school to be used for training or in construction projects that were part of the curriculum.

- The branch manager was invited to see the students in action as they built a model home on their campus as part of the carpentry program.

The bottom line was a strong win for both parties. The branch manager had face-to-face interaction with the students, which provided a clear indication of those who were interested in the restoration business and those who displayed leadership qualities. Over the subsequent couple of years, the contractor hired four or five people who came through the program. The technical school now had a source of information for their students and staff regarding another industry with a need for their skills, in addition to typical construction or remodeling.

Business owners and leaders should continually seek out opportunities to raise the level of awareness of the industry they serve and to promote local business needs and career options. Actions taken now can help build a pipeline that will aid in ensuring the consistent availability of properly educated young people who may choose to pursue a career in your industry. In addition, community exposure to your brand will provide benefits well beyond hiring. Potential customers will be more familiar with your business and referral sources and partner organizations will know you.

Vocational Awareness

Communication regarding career opportunities within the industry and the skills and education required must be focused on both educators and parents. In many cases, the parent's vision is for their child to earn a four-year college degree. It isn't too early to engage in conversations with parents of 13- to 15-year-olds to educate them on the opportunities and earning potential for trades-based careers. Access to parents through public and private secondary school systems can help to relieve bias against the trades as career options for their children and shape curriculum choices through secondary education.

Ensuring that educators are well informed regarding the industry, career opportunities, and earnings potential is the first step toward the discussion of the required skills and curriculum content necessary to support workforce needs.

Not all of the following options are practical for all companies, as some of them are better suited for larger, more established organizations.

Trade Schools and Technical Centers

There are a number of ways for your business and your people to support these relationships and help their programs to remain aligned with your needs.

- Maintain relationships and contact with administrators and those with responsibility for program content. This will help to keep the curriculum aligned with industry and local business needs.

- Donate materials and tools.

- Volunteer for a board position.

- Serve as a guest speaker or instructor.

- Support efforts to provide apprenticeships and internships.

Topics for meetings with technical, trade, or vocational institution contacts include:

- New services, techniques, equipment, and processes that your industry is using.

- Feedback on preparedness and performance of past graduates who have been hired.

- Discussion of opportunities for specific training or demonstrations that could be provided by your company.

- Equipment, tools, or other needs of the school that your company may donate or help arrange to supply through a strategic partnership.

- Disbursement of available scholarship funds. Surely even a nominal scholarship donation would open a door to present at a board meeting or student meeting.

- Opportunities for internships or apprenticeships with your company.

- Events and opportunities for guest speakers and presentations where your company may choose to participate.

In addition to pipeline-building relationships with organizations involved in training and educating potential employees, more general public relations actions should be part of your company's annual plan. The following are a few options for helping people to become familiar with your business and your industry.

Open Houses

A low-cost option for providing increased exposure to your business, the industry, available careers, and the sense of purpose that goes along with helping people in need on a daily basis is hosting an open house. Market a "come when you can" event planned for a specific day that may include some or all of the following options:

- Demonstrations or short training sessions held at scheduled times.

- Tours of the facility.

- A keynote speaker to draw attendees.

- Having the event held in conjunction with a charitable organization and/or fundraiser. One example is to participate in a blood drive where a mobile donation center is onsite during the event.

- Getting your business partners to join in sponsoring the event. These could be customers, suppliers, or referral sources with whom you work.

- Participation by technical or vocational schools that can use the opportunity to create awareness for their programs and explain how they partner with you to help prepare talent for the industry.

Sharing Expertise Through Training

Training that is provided by you and your employees is another vehicle for raising the level of awareness of the industry and your individual business and career opportunities. Actively seek out and promote opportunities to provide free classes and demonstrations at venues like:

- DIY and contractor supply businesses

- Trade and vocational schools

- Career fairs

- Chamber of Commerce and local business promotional events

Strategic Partnerships

Involving companies you work with—or whose equipment, supplies, and materials you use—in joint promotional activities and co-op advertising is another option for spreading the word about your business and reducing your cost for public relations. Think about including these partners when opportunities arise:

- **Vendors**—organizations from which you source services, IT hardware and support, marketing materials, content, and technology.

- **Manufacturers**—tools, vehicles, and equipment.

- **Suppliers**—companies where you purchase construction materials, PPE, tools, vehicles, and equipment.

- **Subcontractors**—partners whom you work with on customer jobs.

For those who want to go a bit deeper into public relations opportunities, we recommend that you seek out occasions to participate in:

- Writing or contributing articles to local newspapers and community newsletters.

- Having employees volunteer for projects like Habitat for Humanity.

- Doing interviews as part of radio broadcasts.

- Participating in career days at local middle schools and high schools.

- Creating podcasts on topics related to the industry and career education.

- Television shows like "Undercover Boss." While this is an extreme example, those who have participated have contributed significantly to increasing awareness of their industry and their company.

Tracking Progress

It is important to be able to track performance to measure the impact of changes you have made that are pertinent to the subject of trade promotion. When using these or other key performance indicators to track performance improvement, be sure to measure your current performance, perhaps going back in time a year or two, to set a baseline. Then track the same metrics after you implement your changes to verify that you are achieving the intended results.

In your annual business planning process, include setting targets or goals for the coming year for the chosen metrics. Here are some examples:

Educational Organizations—number of hours invested in meetings, in-class presentations, and board participation.

Industry Promotion—total number of man hours invested by employees in trade fairs, industry association meetings, and conferences and events that promote your industry.

Promotional Training—number of hours of training provided by your employees to students, career fair attendees, DIY sessions, and other business promotional events.

Joint Advertising—dollars invested in joint promotional activities and co-op advertising during the past year divided by total revenue for the same period.

CHAPTER 15

Conclusion

In writing this book, it was not our intention to suggest you drop everything else you have going on and focus exclusively on what you need to do to attract and retain the best people. If you've owned a business for any length of time, you already know there are many things that demand your attention and that will influence the ultimate success or failure of your business. Still, none of them are more important than populating your company with the right people.

Every day you have challenges and problems that demand your immediate attention: conversations that can't wait until tomorrow; profits to be made; cash to be collected; employees to be hired and trained (or perhaps discharged); payrolls to meet; and quality and service standards to exceed.

In addition to these daily demands, there are forces affecting your business: competitive pressures from other companies in your market; constantly shifting customer expectations and demands; economic pressures; governmental regulatory issues; and even your own health and well-being. But all of these can be handled more effectively by improving the quality and cultural fit of the people on your team.

Surrounding yourself with "A" players is at the heart of what this book is designed to help you do. As I'm sure you've gathered, "A" players is a term I've used to describe strong, competent people who are willing to speak the truth to authority. While this is helpful in every area of life, it's particularly important in business.

Your most important role is to create the culture—the environment that attracts the right people and brings them into your company. Champion your company's commitment to employee development. Maintain the long-term view that will ensure continuity in leadership and the availability of the resources needed to enable your business to reach your vision for its successful future.

The larger our business grows, the more insulated we become from hearing the things that we need to hear from our people. They may feel we're unapproachable or that we think we're above receiving feedback, so they stop offering it. Regardless of the reason, this does nothing but lead to a company's ultimate decline. This is all the more reason for surrounding ourselves with highly competent people who are willing to challenge us and help us recognize how our own personality, management style, and habits may be limiting them and the company.

Lasting change takes time and sustained effort. Quick fixes to deeply ingrained cultures and practices usually don't last. But you can start by taking small steps at improvement. Consistently put one foot in front of the other. Prioritize. Focus on one or two of these chapters to address the changes that are most needed in your organization. Move the needle at least a little bit with every decision or with every change implemented. Celebrate your small improvements. Learn from your setbacks. Keep moving forward. If you don't see remarkable changes in your business overnight, don't get discouraged. Over time, you surely will.

Entrepreneurs are famous for being strong starters, but weak finishers. Too many initiatives fall apart because the owner gets bogged down in details, loses interest, or gets bored and moves onto the next new thing. When change and growth are desired, rekindle the entrepreneurial spirit that helped you create your business in the first place.

Stay the course. Investing in your people is the highest yield option, even though it takes time. Making lasting change within an organization is a marathon, not a sprint. The results, like compound interest, can be powerful even though the rewards are reaped down the road.

You've already gotten a start by reading this book. Now, take the next step and download the online Appendix documents by visiting business-expertpress.com, then searching for Violand. Keep moving forward, and good luck on your journey.

About the Author

Chuck Violand is the founder and principal of Violand Management Associates (VMA), a consulting company working internationally throughout the United States, Canada, and Australia, whose focus is on small businesses.

Chuck started VMA in 1987 to help small businesses achieve sustained profitable growth and to help their owners and management teams achieve long-term professional and personal success.

As an author and popular keynote speaker, Chuck is a respected authority on the unique challenges faced by entrepreneurial small businesses, having spent over 30 years as a business consultant and an executive coach. He is a regular contributor to trade publications and newsletters in addition to authoring his popular, weekly leadership series *Monday Morning Notes*.

In his more than 50 years of owning businesses, Chuck's varied experiences include having owned nightclubs, a food processing company, and contracting companies. Today, he continues to play an active role at VMA.

Index

OTHER TITLES IN THE HUMAN RESOURCE MANAGEMENT AND ORGANIZATIONAL BEHAVIOR COLLECTION

Michael J. Provitera, Barry University, Editor

- *11 Secrets of Nonprofit Excellence* by Kathleen Stauffer
- *The Nonprofit Imagineers* by Ben Vorspan
- *At Home With Work* by Nyla Naseer
- *Improv to Improve Your Leadership Team* by Candy Campbell
- *Leadership In Disruptive Times* by Sattar Bawany
- *The Intrapreneurship Formula* by Sandra Lam
- *Navigating Conflict* by Lynne Curry
- *Innovation Soup* by Sanjay Puligadda and Don Waisanen
- *The Aperture for Modern CEOs* by Sylvana Storey
- *The Future of Human Resources* by Tim Baker
- *Change Fatigue Revisited* by Richard Dool and Tahsin I. Alam
- *Championing the Cause of Leadership* by Ted Meyer
- *Embracing Ambiguity* by Michael Edmondson
- *Breaking the Proactive Paradox* by Tim Baker
- *The Modern Trusted Advisor* by Nancy MacKay and Alan Weiss

Concise and Applied Business Books

The Collection listed above is one of 30 business subject collections that Business Expert Press has grown to make BEP a premiere publisher of print and digital books. Our concise and applied books are for...

- Professionals and Practitioners
- Faculty who adopt our books for courses
- Librarians who know that BEP's Digital Libraries are a unique way to offer students ebooks to download, not restricted with any digital rights management
- Executive Training Course Leaders
- Business Seminar Organizers

Business Expert Press books are for anyone who needs to dig deeper on business ideas, goals, and solutions to everyday problems. Whether one print book, one ebook, or buying a digital library of 110 ebooks, we remain the affordable and smart way to be business smart. For more information, please visit www.businessexpertpress.com, or contact sales@businessexpertpress.com.

Printed in the USA
CPSIA information can be obtained
at www.ICGtesting.com
JSHW052346230524
63525JS00003B/14